STORES
AND RETAIL SPACES

**FROM THE INSTITUTE OF STORE PLANNERS
AND THE EDITORS OF VM+SD**

ST PUBLICATIONS
CINCINNATI, OHIO

ISBN: 0-944094-29-5

Published by:
ST Publications, Inc.
Book Division
407 Gilbert Avenue
Cincinnati, Ohio 45202
Tel. 513-421-2050
Fax 513-421-6110

Distributed to the book and art trade in the U.S. and Canada by:
Watson-Guptill Publications
1515 Broadway
New York, NY 10036
Tel. 908-363-4511
Fax 908-363-0338

Distributed to the rest of the world by:
Hearst Books International
1350 Avenue of the Americas
New York, NY 10003
Tel. 212-261-6770
Fax 212-261-6795

Book design by Carole Winters
Art production by Rhinoworks, Cincinnati

On the cover: Hudon's Somerset Collection, Troy, Michigan. Photo: Chun Y Lai, New York City
Back cover photos: Lucy Chen, Somerville, Mass. (top); Dub Rogers, New York City (middle);
Elliott Kaufman, New York City (bottom)

Printed in Hong Kong

10 9 8 7 6 5 4 3 2 1

INTRODUCTION

Publication of STORES AND RETAIL SPACES marks the third cooperative product between VM+SD magazine and the Institute of Store Planners (ISP). In this volume, the editors of VM+SD have compiled the most significant projects of 1997 and 1998 in cooperation with ISP. These award-winning projects were determined by a panel distinguished judges who viewed more than 300 submissions. Evaluated on five qualities: planning and design, lighting, visual merchandising, graphics and innovation, the stores on the following pages exemplify these aspects at the highest level.

Through photographs and floorplans, STORES AND RETAIL SPACE presents the most current thinking in retail design. You'll also find the latest in materials, technology and techniques in planning along with environmental graphics that are so critical in creating retail brands. Examples range from traditional department and specialty stores to mass merchants and supermarkets to the brave new realm of entertainment retailing.

The elements of great store design bring influences and trends from around the world and across cultures to create successful shopping environments — ones that suit the merchandise, the community, and, most importantly, the customer.

In assembling the environments and materials of some of the best, VM+SD offers a volume from which to draw ideas, innovation and inspiration, not only for store designers and planners, but for all involved in the beauty and science of selling.

Janet Groeber

Editor/Associate Publisher

VM+SD — Visual Merchandising and Store Design magazine

CONTENTS

HOLT RENFREW
TORONTO

The exterior entrance of Holt Renfrew's Yorkdale store sets the tone for simplicity inside - modern and classic contemporary. Pale backgrounds and virtually transparent fixtures create a sense of elegant openness throughout the 45,000-square-foot store. Colors are cool, pale blues and greens on many wall surfaces, echoed by edge-mounted, frosted-acrylic partitions and departmental signs that seem to float in space. Elsewhere, wall panels fade from green or blue into shell-pink, and opalescent floral patterns appear at the base of walls. A variety of visual textures greet shoppers as well – walls are smooth, but balanced by columns wrapped in sculpted plaster.

In the shoe department, illuminated wall niches display shoes and accessories creating a checkerboard. The wall is used to highlight "leading-edge" items as a preview of coming attractions. Muted colors emphasize the contrast in textures.

Design: Yabu Pushelberg, Toronto – George Yabu, creative director; Glenn Pushelberg, managing partner; Chris Koroknay, studio director; Tara Browne, marketing director; Janis Chow, senior designer; Doug Wilson, project manager; Polly Chan, designer; Gary Chan, designer; Christina Gustavs, designer; Michelle Culjat, designer; Anthony Tey, architectural technologist Holt Renfrew design team: Joel Rath, president; Jim Brandl, executive vice president and ceo; Anne Walker, vice president for construction and design; Peter Lawrence, regional manager for visual merchandising Architecture: Pellow + Associates Architects Inc., Toronto General Contractor: Scepter Industries, Toronto Video: Greneker, Los Angeles Fixturing: Erik Cabinets, Hamilton, Ont.; Unique Store Fixtures, Concord, Ont.; Provincial Store Fixtures, Malton, Ont. Hardware: Universal Showcase, Woodbridge, Ont. Furniture: Louis Interiors, Toronto; Nienkamper/ICF, Toronto; Keilhauer, Scarborough, Ont.; Knoll, New York City; Palazzetti, Long Island City, N.Y. Flooring: Elte Carpets, Toronto; Enmar Natural Stone, Concord, Ont.; Marbletrend, Toronto Lighting: Eurolite, Toronto Special finishes: Moss + Lam, Toronto Plaster work: Plasterform, Mississauga, Ont. Wallcoverings: Metro Wallcovering, Concord, Ont. ceilings: New Generation Group, Toronto

Photography by Robert Burley, Design Archive, Toronto

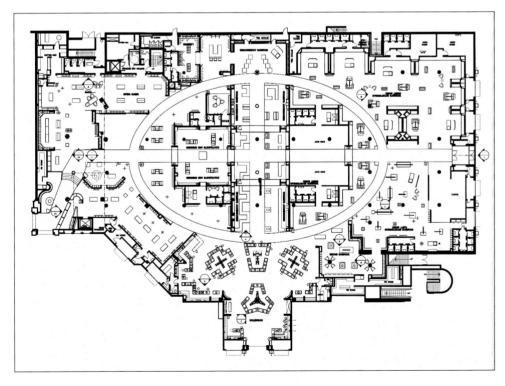

SOKOS
HELSINKI

The redefining of the downtown Helsinki department store called for SOKOS to be repositioned as an affordable fashion retailer where a family could shop together, requiring an expansion of product lines to include lifestyle items. The landmark building was redesigned to include an atrium running from the second floor to the sixth. The atrium creates visual interest by opening up the store, adding light, movement and space. SOKOS' "Back to Basics" strategy was underlined through the use of natural finishes such as limestone, wood and ceramic throughout the store. A new layout for fashion departments encourages men and women to shop together by designing each floor to reflect the clothing offered. Simplifying the shopping experience by keeping the lifestyle of the target customer at the core of the product offerings was a goal of the design team.

Design: Retail Planning Associates, Columbus, Ohio – Doug Cheesman, chair; Mike Gilling, design director; Jeff McCall, retail strategist; Sam Biddlecombe and Giles Brookes, interior designers; John Barber, architect; Marie Haines, merchandiser; Perry Kotick, lighting designer; Andy Dorman, Russell Holmes and Victoria Ward, graphic designers; Jason Puddefoot, visual communications SOKOS Team: Harri Laaksonen, retail planning manager; Heikki Karttunen, Pekka Saaskilahti, Keijo Pennanen Architect: KY, Helsinki Fixturing: Umdasch GmbH, Austria

Photography by Chris Gascoigne, England

GALERIES LAFAYETTE
BERLIN

In introducing Galeries Lafayette as the benchmark of style to a German audience, design of the new Berlin store features an impressive central atrium consisting of a large cone pointing up from the ground floor into the lower floor and parking floor. Five selling floors, relatively small in size, are located around a major circular aisle. Themes of each floor — colors, materials, images and forms — are based on individual French masterpiece paintings. Floor coverings, for example, mix bright terrazzo with subdued tones of marble and granite, while simple metal, wood and glass details on fixtures add to the clean and ordered environment. As part of the store's "French-ness," a Weekend in Paris information kiosk with touch screens provides customers with travel and cultural information about France; and a video wall shows French films. Fashion counseling and personal shopping services are also available, as in the Paris store.

Design: WalkerGroup/CNI, New York City — Mark Bradin, vice president and principal-in-charge; Martin Jerry, vice president and creative director; Jorgen Engersgard, project designer; Howard Pasternack, senior designer; Glennys Anglada, graphic designer; Jed Clifford, CADD operator Galeries Lafayette (Paris) team: Yves Auberty, managing director; Daniel Mourlot, store planning and design director; Monique Cussac, design coordinator Architect of Record: Klaus Effenberger Architect, Berlin General contractor: CBC, ParisFixtures: Dula, Dortmund, Germany

Photography by Dub Rogers, New York City

HUDSON'S, SOMERSET COLLECTION

TROY, MICH.

A point of reference for each level, the monumental atrium at the heart of this 300,000-sq.-ft. Hudson's includes signature lighting details and a European glass clock. Around the atrium, sleek focal walls of light wood and glass lead into designer boutiques and provide space for changing fashion presentations. Within the open plan, designer shops including DKNY are defined by wood and glass slab "theater walls" and signature fixtures. In the Oval Room, fine women's fashions are presented in a proscenium-arched space with hand-tufted carpets and pale anigre walls. The store also includes the "FYI" personal shopper service in an elegant, elliptical salon; dramatically lighted fur salon that incorporates fine furniture and museum-quality artwork; Juniors' department with a "bar-style" circular cashwrap; and Grand Cosmetics Hall with high ceilings, detailed columns, warm woods and cream marble floors.

Design: The Pavlik Design Team, Ft. Lauderdale, Fla. — Ronald J. Pavlik, president/ ceo; Lucia Diaz, project manager; Luis Valladares, director of design; Fernando Castillo, project designer; Placido Herrera, project designer; Cesar Lucero, planner Retailer's team: Dayton Hudson Department Store Co., Minneapolis — Andrew Markopoulos, senior vice president of visual merchandising and store design (retired); Ray Steffner, vice president properties; Jane Carrott-Van Auken, director, store planning and design; Jamie Becker, director, visual merchandising; Floyd Zdrojkowski, director, construction Architect: Greiner Inc., Minneapolis General contractor: Hudsons Construction, Troy, Mich. Fixturing: MET Merchandising, Chicago; Otema Store Fixtures, Markham, Ont. Lighting: Manning Lighting, Sheboygan, Wis. Laminates: Wilsonart, Temple, Texas; Formica, Cincinnati; Pionite, Auburn, Maine; Westinghouse Micarta, Hampton, S.C. Wall coverings: Design Tex, Woodside, N.Y.; Innovations in Wallcoverings, New York City; Maya Romanoff, Chicago; Silk Dynasty, Mt. View, Calif. Fabrics: B. Berger Co., Macedonia, Ohio; Brunschwig & Fils, New York City; Carnegie, Rockville Centre, N.Y.; Groves Brothers Fabrics, Ft. Worth, Texas; Payne Fabrics, Dayton, Ohio; J. Robert Scott & Associates, Los Angeles

Photography by Chun Y Lai, New York City

IWATAYA Z-SIDE

FUKUOKA, JAPAN

This Japanese department store is designed around carefully thought-out concepts of names and icons, closely tied to key design signatures and materials to create strong identities for each floor. The main floor, with a architecturally influenced flower icon, is called "Style Perfection"; colors, patterns and materials throughout the floor accessorize the natural landscape. The men's floor, using a knight symbol, is named "Simple Sophistication," while "Gourmet Satisfaction" denotes the food floor. Young fashions and women's shoes are on the "X Generation" floor, characterized by an X symbol and collages of images communicating the vitality, attitude, image and lifestyle of its target customers.

Design: WalkerGroup/CNI, New York City — Mark Bradin, account executive; Martin Jerry, vice president, creative designer; Peter Scavuzzo, vice president, graphic design; Milosh Sekulich, project executive; Yoshi Shiraishi, project designer; Christina Walker, senior graphic designer; Harua Uekusa, design coordinator; Tak Tsukahara, project coordinator Iwataya's team: Kenichi Nakamuta, president; Yasuo Ishii, vice president; Masamichi Furusawa, vice chief of strategic planning center; Jiro Oda, managing director of merchandising; Hideaki Shinozaki, general manager and project coordinator Architect: WalkerGroup/CNI

Photography by Dub Rogers, New York City

JOSLINS, PARK MEADOWS MALL
LITTLETON, COLO.

At the client's request, the focal point of the 240,000-square-foot store is its spectacular view of the Rocky Mountains. To capture the view without distracting from the merchandise presentation, the design features a three-story atrium with full-height glass and an observation elevator framed by a heavily textured stone wall. Adding to the "outdoor" feel of the structure are two 55-foot glass waterfalls cascading into a rock pool. The amount of daylight streaming into the selling areas is filtered by the escalators, which cross in a giant "X" immediately inside the window, allowing shoppers a clear view of the scenery while riding, but separating the selling floor from the bright exterior views. In the evening, the atrium and exterior facade are enhanced with a three-hour theatrical lighting sequence visible from both inside and outside the store, transforming what would have been merely a reflective black surface into a dazzling attraction.

Design: CML Design Associates, Coconut Grove, Fla. – Christopher M. Love, designer; Robert Corso, project manager; Nylett Penton, color and materials; David Clark, design Mercantile Stores Company Design Team, Fairfield, Ohio – David Nichols, chair and ceo; Randolph Burnett, senior vice president of real estate; Ronald Gosses, vice president of visual merchandise; Mary Ann Berting, Lynn Larson and Sandy Rice – visual team; Bruce Quisno, director of real estate facilities; Lori Kolthoff, manager of store design; Earl Carpenter, manager of store planning; Marty Weldishofer and Mike Daly – store planning; Pam Henegar, purchasing; Mike Hill, manager of construction; Bob King, project manager; Carl Necaise, lighting. Credits continued on p.173.

Photography by Ron Forth Photography, Boulder, Colo.(p.20) and Richard K. Loesch, New Albany, Ohio (p.21)

MARSHALL FIELD'S

WATERTOWER PLACE, CHICAGO

The renovation of this 284,000-square-foot Marshall Field's first floor and mezzanine transformed the cosmetics area into a Parisian boulevard flanked by shops. Columns and chandeliers are crowned with a cove-lit ceiling running the full length of the store to create a "light court" of the now-unified first floor and curved balconies of the mezzanine. Opening the escalator well made possible a stepped space between the escalators for seasonal and visual presentations. On the mezzanine, fashion accessories are set in residential vignettes with fine furnishings and the restored original ivory travertine floor. Light woods, pearl trim and Fortuny-inspired carpeting provide a neutral backdrop. On the eighth floor, home merchandise has been converted from a closed-in shops to an open-plan gallery of fine home collections. Residential, furniture-style fixtures, cream casework and silver-leaf trim are set against taupe carpet and ivory porcelain aisles.

Design: The Pavlik Design Team, Ft. Lauderdale, Fla. — Ronald J. Pavlik, president and ceo; Luis Valladares, director of design; Fernando Castillo, project designer; Placido Herrera, project designer; Cesar Lucero, planner, Lucia Diaz, project manager Dayton Hudson Team: Andrew Markopoulos, senior vice president of visual merchandising and store design (retired); Ray Steffner, vice president properties; Jane Carrott-Van Auken, director, store planning and design; Jamie Becker, director, visual merchandising; Floyd Zdrojkowski, director, construction Architect: Chipman & Adams, Park Ridge, Ill. — Robert Gross, project architect General contractor: Pepper Construction, Chicago — Robert Hosack, project manager Fixturing: Met Merchandising, Chicago; Bernhard Woodwork, Northbrook, Ill. Flooring: Innovative Marble & Tile, Farmingdale, N.Y.; PermaGrain Products, Newtown Square, Pa.; Atlas Carpet Mills, City of Commerce, Calif.; Durkan Patterned Carpet, Dalton, Ga.; Mohawk Commercial Carpet, Atlanta Ceiling: Armstrong, Lancaster, Pa. Lighting: New Metal Crafts, Chicago Laminates: Wilsonart, Temple, Texas; Formica, Cincinnati; Westinghouse Micarta, Hampton, S.C.; Laminart, Elk Grove Village, Ill.; Pioneer Plastics, Auburn, Maine Wall coverings: Innovations in Wallcoverings, New York City; F. Schumacher & Co., New York City

Photography by Myro Rosky, Ft. Lauderdale , Fla.

BARNES & NOBLE JUNIORS DEPARTMENT

UNION SQUARE, NEW YORK CITY

With the intent to establish memorable "boutique style" spaces and departments within the Barnes & Noble store, Kiko Obata introduced separate juniors department identities for scale, wayfinding and accessibility purposes. Illustrated book characters, colorful signage, murals and custom honey maple fixtures distinguish these juniors areas from the darker woods used throughout the rest of the store. Features include a "Front Steps" fixture with book characters on screen-printed maple; a "Reading Porch" new merchandise feature area against a blue-sky mural; and "Pooh's Forest," with its lifesize illustrated trees, provides a stage for storytelling and community activities.

Design: Kiku Obata + Co., St. Louis — Kiku Obata, Idie McGinty, Tim McGinty, Jane McNeely, Theresa Henrekin, Pam Bliss, Kathleen Robert, Liz Sullivan, Joe Floresca, David Hercules, Arden Launius, Lisa Bollman, Kim Tunze, Beth Wall Barnes & Noble team: David Nicholson Architect: By 3 Group, New York City Fixturing/ graphics: Engraphix, St. Louis; Design Fabricators, Boulder, Colo.; RDA, Greenlawn, N.Y.

Photography by Balthazar Korab, Troy, Mich.

NICKELODEON

VIACOM ENTERTAINMENT STORE, CHICAGO

The 6500-square-foot shop occupies a two-story section of the 30,000-square-foot Viacom store, and is designed with many opportunities for hands-on interaction. The two floors are connected by a giant totem that runs up through the ceiling. Punching a button on the totem activates audio and mechanical sequences. A punching column powers a blimp that goes up and down between floors, a "Gak Vat" mixes and bubbles to manufacture gak, a "Hide-Out Hut" made to look like a corrugated box allows kids to spy around the store using a periscope and a variety of "kid-pleasing" audio can be triggered by light beams as customers pass through them. "The Ultimate Room" houses the Nick "at home" products, such as a line of furniture featuring secret compartments to appeal to kids. The "Kids Closet," within the "Ultimate Room," is stuffed with the kinds of things typically found in a kid's closet. Sound effects triggered by the door include crashing pots and pans and laughing Nick characters.

Concept Design: Fitch Inc., Worthington, Ohio — Mark Artus, project manager; Christian Davies and Melissa Smith-Hazen, associate vice presidents; Paul Lechleiter, vice president; Lisa Justus and Steve Pottschmidt, associates; Doug Smith and Lynn Rosenbaum, directors Viacom Retail Group, Store Development, Dallas — Lori Wegman, vice president of store development; Robert Anthony, director of media technology; Brian Cornelius, director of store development; Eric Corti, director of construction management; Mary Martel, manager of visual merchandise; Jane McNeely, director of graphics and scenic design Architect: FRCH Design Worldwide Media Technology Consultant: Edwards Technology, El Segundo, Calif. General Contractor: Capital Construction, Wheeling, Ill. Fixturing: FHC, Chicago; Design Fabricators, Lafayette, Colo. Flooring: Arrow Patterned Concrete, Bloomington, Ill. Signage and Graphics: Environmental Design, St. Louis; Skyline Design, Chicago; Whiteway Signs, Chicago; X Design, Columbus, Ohio Scenic Design: Joel Klaff, Chicago; Nick Studios, Orlando; TW Design, Houston Media Technology: Eastman Kodak, Rochester, N.Y.; Muze, New York City

Photography by Dan Forer, Chicago

I.N.C. INT'L. CONCEPTS VENDOR SHOP

NEW YORK CITY

When Federated Merchandise Services created the I.N.C. Int'l. private-label line of apparel for young, active women, it was with an emphasis on wardrobe planning for work and leisure. The shops, which will roll out to Federated department stores in key markets, will be based on this prototype by Robert Young Associates. Arranged around a "runway" main axis, the 5,500-square-foot shop incorporates clean-lined, international-style stainless steel fixtures with natural mahogany and leather accents. Sisal-like carpet and green stone in the hard-surface flooring add warmth. A circular band of signage is independent of the back wall, above two crescent-shaped cashwraps where customers can sit and consult with an I.N.C. specialist.

Design: Robert Young Associates, Dallas — Thomas Herndon, principal in charge; Ramsay Weatherford, project planner; John Von Mohr, project designer; Tommy Nelson, project manager Macy's team: Joseph Feczko, senior vice president of marketing; Karen Wenzel-Murphy, vice president of store development and visual Fixturing: Toledo Store Fixtures, Toledo, Ohio; Dooge Veneers, Grand Rapids, Mich. Furniture: Goodman Charlton, Dallas Flooring: Innovative Tile & Marble, Farmingdale, N.Y. Lighting: Indy Lighting, Indianapolis Graphics: Modern Age Photography, New York City; Seven Continents, Toronto (frame) Props/decoratives: David Sunderland, Dallas (bongo stools) Mannequins/forms: Goldsmith, Long Island City, N.Y.; Seven Continents, Toronto (base)

Photography by Elliott Kaufman, New York City

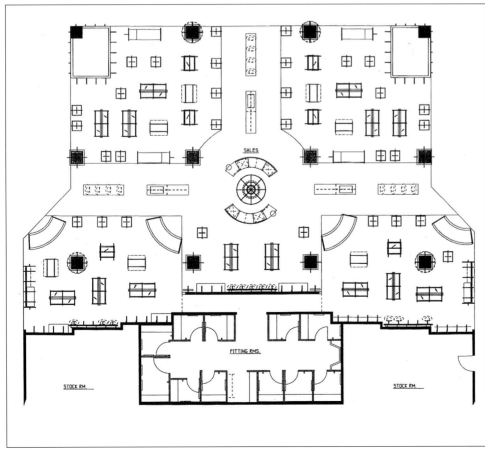

ERNO LASZLO

EATON'S, EATON CENTRE, TORONTO

In updating the prototype for the Erno Laszlo skin care line, the client's objectives were to continue the loyalty of existing clients, to increase awareness among cosmetics and skin care purchasers, to emphasize the professional aesthetic services and to project the long tradition of the Swiss skin care line. The design, planned to be restrained yet evocative and dramatic, was to expand the vendor's presence from a ten-foot counter to a 20-foot counter and add two 100-square-foot "cabines" for facials. The damage-resistant counter area also had to accommodate two areas for customers to meet with skin care consultants. The designers opted for a curvilinear feel in the expansion area, maximizing perimeter service counter space while allowing for seating in the consulting areas at the showcase ends. A monochromatic scheme, ranging from warm shades of taupe to clean whites with white-washed maple, predominates the space, along with flesh-toned maple used with satin nickel and black trim for wall and floor fixtures. The back wall fixtures are outlined in squares of satin nickel and lit by fluorescent lamps behind satin glass. Matte black graphics are employed for the fret cut and pierced lettering and the trademark screen-printed angel head logo to evoke a late twenties feel.

Design: Fiorino Design Inc., Toronto — Nella Fiorino, principal; Vilija Gacionis, interior designer Erno Laszlo Team: Penny Tadeka, director General Contractor: Sajo Construction Inc., Montreal Furniture: Beaton Agencies, Toronto Lighting: Lightolier, Fall River, Mass. Laminates: Wilsonart International, Temple, Texas; Nevamar International Paper, Odenton, Md. Wall Coverings: Benjamin Moore & Co. Ltd., Montvale, N.J. Fabrics: Lauriitex, Toronto Signage & Graphics: Sunset Neon, Burlington, Ont.

Photography by Robert Burley, Design Archive, Toronto

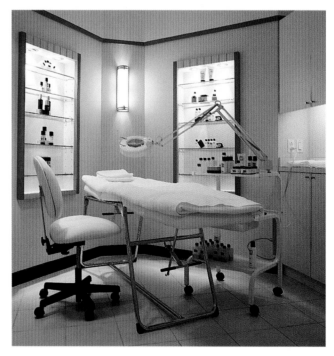

LEFT BANK

HOLT RENFREW, TORONTO

Holt Renfrew's fashion-forward private-label shop balances a subdued palette of cream, silver and cool blue against the vivid graphic appeal of sixties and seventies design. Illuminated acrylic walls and custom freestanding fixtures divide the 4,500-square-foot space into merchandising niches for designer lines. Concave ceiling "dishes" alternate with custom downlighting and provide a subtle counterpoint with the painted concrete floor patterns. Holt Renfrew plans to roll out this prototype design to additional store renovations in Canada.

Design: Yabu Pushelberg, Toronto — Glenn Pushelberg, George Yabu, Tara Browne, Belinda Wong, Gary Chan, Polly Chan, Anthony Tey Holt Renfrew team: Anne Walker, vice president of design and construction; Rochelle Jones, design manager General contractor: Pickett Construction Management, Toronto Fixturing: Unique Store Fixtures, Concord, Ont. Furniture: Full House, New York City Flooring: Moss & Lam, Toronto Ceiling: Formglas, Toronto Lighting: Lightolier, Secaucus, N.J. Materials: Cyro Canada, Mississauga, Ont. (acrylic) Wall coverings: Metro Wallcovering, Concord, Ont. Fabrics: Primavera, Toronto Signage: Wilcox Sign Co., Toronto

Photography by Robert Burley, Design Archive, Toronto

SPECTTICA FASHION OPTICIANS

KING OF PRUSSIA, PA.

Taking an upscale yet minimalist approach to eyewear, Lenscrafter's new 1,237-square-foot prototype houses frames, lenses and optometric services for fashion-conscious customers. In a pale-neutral colored interior of marble flooring, rich wood custom fixtures, accented by brushed metal framework, offer a contrast. Oval inserts into wall cases present featured products on glass shelves. Graphics, including backlit metal signage, copper-colored case signage, fashion photography, packaging and labels, continue the minimalist approach to design.

Design: Chute Gerdeman, Columbus, Ohio — Phil White, project designer, architecture and interior design; Dennis Gerdeman, ceo; Susan Hessler, project designer, graphics and signage Lenscrafter team: Traci Hahn-Dyer, project leader; Renee Ritter, Jim Henessey, Becky Clifton-Lagore; Kerry Pickett, Lou Beckmeyer, design team Architect: White Associates Architects, Columbus, Ohio Fixturing/furniture: OSF America, Columbus, Ohio Paint: Polomyx, Cambridge, Mass. Signage: Artglo Co., Columbus, Ohio

Photography by Brian Steege, Guildhaus Photographic, Cincinnati

EYE-X

COLUMBIA MALL, COLUMBIA, MD.

Sunglass Hut's Eye-X concept targets affluent customers who want stylish, contemporary prescription eyewear. Design called for a 670-square-foot loft-type space with natural materials, including weathered metal and a wood floor, for comfort. The "X" logo is echoed throughout the store, beginning with the storefront window and continuing to small vitrines attached to "X"-shaped braces and cross-legged occasional tables. Shelf-style wall fixturing of plywood and reconstituted wood veneer, backlit with fluorescent lighting fixtures, is crowned with a decorative wood treatment that also incorporates the logo. Wood flooring and ceiling treatments pick up the metal detailing, with metal-clad ceiling beams and copper-tone metal plates in the center of the floor.

Design: Michel Dubuc Concept Inc., Montreal — Michel Dubuc, principal in charge; Fabien Nadeau, senior project designer; Marie-Claude Demers, project manager Sunglass Hut team: Fran Anderson, project manager; Susan Yost, vice president of merchandising Architect: Dennis Mitchell, AIA, Arlington, Texas General contractor: James Barb Construction, Albuquerque, N.M. Fixturing: National Store Fixtures and Display, Pompano Beach, Fla. Flooring: RJ Pitcher, Liverpool, N.Y. (wood); Associated Carpets, New York City (limestone) Lighting: FCA Electric, Weehawken, N.J. Storefront: D&R Glass Inc., Ontario, Calif. Signage: Triangle Signs, Baltimore

Photography by Elliott Kaufman, New York City

COMCAST COMMUNICATIONS CENTER

KING OF PRUSSIA, PA.

The center is organized with a series of arches that lure shoppers into the store and lead them to a nine-screen video wall at the rear of the space. The arches divide the store into zones for each of Comcast's entities: cellular, interactive and entertainment. The open ceiling and walls are painted dark blue to allow the casework and arches to "float in space." The perimeter of the store is lined with repetitive fixtures slightly angled to stimulate interest without overwhelming the rhythm of the store. Theatrical light fixtures are supported on floating rings above each interactive station.

Design: Charles E. Broudy & Associates, Philadelphia — Charles Broudy, president; David Schwing, design; Michael Broudy, project manager; Edward Einhouse and Carl Gutilla, project team Comcast Metrophone Team, Wayne, Pa. — Craig Murphy, director of retail operations Electrical Engineer: Steven Shore, P.E., Bala Cynwyd, Pa. Mechanical Engineer: Richard Kates, P.E., Merion, Pa. General Contractor: Wolfe Scott Associates, Philadelphia Furniture: Carnegie, Rockville Centre, N.Y. Fixturing: Phoenix Wood Products, Niagara Falls, Ont. Specialty Metalwork: CB Metal Industries, Inc., Downsview, Ont. Laminates: Pionite Decorative Laminates, Auburn, Maine; Wilsonart International, Temple, Texas; Lamin-Art, Elk Grove Village, Ill. Flooring: Patcraft Commercial Carpet, a division of Queen Carpet Corporation, Dalton, Ga.; Roman Mosaic and Tile Co., West Chester, Pa. Wall Coverings: Duron, King of Prussia, Pa.; Chroma-Spec; Artisitic Coatings, Prospect Park, Pa.; Golterman and Sabo, St. Louis Fabrics: Carnegie, Rockville Centre, N.Y.; Pallas Textiles, Green Bay, Wis. Signage and Graphics: Capitol Sign Systems, Landsdale, Pa.; Silberman Group, West Chester, Pa.; Burton Photo, Philadelphia Fiberoptics: Fiberoptics International, Seattle Audio-Visual, Lighting, Sound Control: Showorks Audio-Visual, Wilmington, Del. Vinyl Base: Johnsonite, Chagrin Falls, Ohio Acoustic Ceiling: Armstrong World Industries, Lancaster, Pa. Interactive Touchscreens: Frontier, Malvern, Pa.

Photography by Matt Wargo, Philadelphia

ELECTRONIC INNOVATIONS

HARTSFIELD ATLANTA INT'L. AIRPORT, ATLANTA

Providing electronic accessories to the modern traveler, Electronic Innovations' design imagery evolved from the combination of two themes — travel and electronics. Gadget display fixture design, for example, suggests technological devices, while display niches are backed by "circuit-board" green metal. Hovering over the 540-square-foot space, a skeletal airplane wing communicates the travel aspect of the store, as do the riveted aircraft metal "skin" on the walls and the aircraft cable that suspends glass shelves of multimedia products. Niches are topped by changeable p-o-p category signs and products stored in locked cases are displayed on flexible display walls that permit interactivity.

Design: Miroglio Architecture + Design, Oakland, Calif. — Joel Miroglio, designer Retailer's team: Jay and Arthur Richardson, owners Architect: Miroglio Architecture + Design General contractor: Tandem Contracting Inc., Marietta, Ga. Fixturing: Trinity Engineering, Rohnert Park, Calif. Flooring: Atlas Carpet, City of Commerce, Calif. Ceiling: Armstrong, Chicago Lighting: Tech Lighting, Chicago Laminates: Abet Laminati, Teterboro, N.J. Signage: Capital Signs, Atlanta

Photography by Robert Thien Photography, Atlanta

EYEWORLD

CAMBRIDGESIDE GALLERIA, CAMBRIDGE, MASS.

The deep, narrow space split by a line of columns running the length of the space at the Cambridgeside Galleria posed a unique challenge to the design team, whose goals were to update the finishes and fixtures, maximize the use of large-capacity tiered display fixtures and incorporate a cable display system. In addition, the team was charged with updating EyeWorld's signage and graphics, improving product presentation and lighting and giving the store a more residential feel. The "EyeWorld" blue trademark, previously used only on stationery, was introduced to reinforce corporate identity and to provide color in the otherwise neutral environment. Transparent graphics lend an eyeglass-like delicacy and airiness to the space, contrasting with the massive size of the signage above. Materials throughout are consistent with those of eyewear: glass, wood and metal. Fixtures were refinished and altered to fit the new prototype design, and residential-inspired dispensing tables and seating emphasize customer comfort.

Design: Bergmeyer Associates, Inc., Boston – David Tubridy, AIA, president; Lewis Muhlfelder, AIA, principal-in-charge; Raymond Mitrano, AIA, project manager; Matthew Hyatt, RA, designer; Kerry Sevigny, designer Eyeworld Team: Rick Simoneau, director lab operations & site; Yulia Nemirovsky, vice president of merchandising; Karen Shekofsky, graphic designer Architect: Bergmeyer Associates, Inc., Boston General Contractor: Union Construction, Lowell, Mass. Fixturing: B&N Industries, San Carlos, Calif.; Hafele, Archdale, N.C. Furniture: Bernhardt, Lenoir, N.C.; A.G.I., High Point, N.C. Flooring: Permagrain, Newtown, Pa.; Durkan Patterned Carpet, Inc., Dalton, Ga. Lighting: Lightolier, Fall River, Mass.; L.B.L., Chicago Heights, Ill. Laminates: Arborite, Hazelton, Pa.; Formica Corporation, Cincinnati; Wilsonart International, Temple, Texas Wall Coverings: Benjamin Moore & Co. Ltd., Montvale, N.J. Signage: Sunshine Sign Company, N. Grafton, Mass.

Photography by Lucy Chen, Somerville, Mass.

POTTERY BARN

BACKBAY HISTORICAL DISTRICT, BOSTON

For the Newbury Street store, the design team worked with the Back Bay Historical Commission to create a design sensitive to the historic character of the location. The existing cast bronze and wood facade was restored, while modern signage and prototypical Pottery Barn cast stone storefront bases were employed to showcase the Pottery Barn identity. The historic character of the existing interior space was merged with the retailer's prototypical elements. Pressed tin ceiling panels and ornate cove moldings introduce the ornamentation typical of a building of this period, while the trademark Pottery Barn concrete and wood floors incorporate a modern aesthetic element. Custom-designed light fixtures and steel and fir display fixtures create a balance between rough and warm finishes.

Design: McCall Design Group, San Franisco – Michael McCall, principal; Carol Curren, project manager; Stan Eastland, project architect Pottery Barn Team: Bud Cope, director of store planning, William-Sonoma, Inc. Architect: Michael McCall, McCall Design Group, San Francisco Lighting Consultants: Ron DeAlessi Lighting Design (storefront lighting), Seattle General Contractor: Fisher Development, Inc., San Francisco Fixturing: Environments, Minnetonka, Minn. Lighting: American Wholesale Lighting, Freemont, Calif. Signage: Thomas Swan Signs, San Francisco

Photography by McCall Design Group, San Francisco

CAMELOT MUSIC

GREAT LAKES MALL, MENTOR, OHIO

When the mall-based Camelot Music chain decided to open a larger, 17,000-square-foot flagship store, the decision was made to compete on platforms of service, experience and technology rather than price. Camelot's broad appeal to music-lovers of all ages included a palette of intense, saturated colors in a cavernous industrial space. Lighting effects reproduce theatrical environments with oscillating track heads and template graphics. Invisible laser technology allows customers to step onto a numbered floor circle to hear top-20 tunes, triggering the audio mechanism to project that particular music through a localized sound dome. Typical music-store long rack fixtures have been replaced by shorter racks, interspersed with cross-merchandising fixtures.

Design: Jon Greenberg & Associates, Southfield, Mich. — Michael Crosson, ceo; Kenneth Nisch, principal in charge; Jenness Anderson, planner/ designer; Michael Benincasa, designer; Edward Kaffel, project manager Camelot team: Kenneth Chance, vice president store planning and operations Architect: Jon Greenberg & Associates, Inc. General contractor: Gaetano Contracting, Canton, Ohio Lighting Design: Illuminating Concepts, Farmington Hills, Mich. Audio/video consultant: AEI Music, Seattle Fixturing: Kason, Binghampton, N.Y. Flooring: Amtico, Glen Ellyn, Ill. Lighting: Kramer Lighting, Fall River, Mass. Ceiling: USG, Chicago; Sequentia, Middleburg Heights, Ohio Graphics: Communication Arts, Boulder, Calif. Mannequins: Greneker, Los Angeles

Photography by Camelot Music, Canton, Ohio

E.L.C. (EARLY LEARNING CENTRE)

KENSINGTON STREET, LONDON

In repositioning the chain of developmental toy stores to appeal to a wider audience, the design team incorporated new logos, color-coded signage and graphics and a number of fictional characters to engage children while defining merchandise categories for their parents. The characters and their story, created by the designers, feature "E.L.C. Kids" and an E.L.C. clubhouse situated in a mythological town where "Professor Bear" and "Sir Bashful Beagle" are always available to lend educational and moral support. Flooring features randomly placed animal inlays to interest children crawling through the store. The team also maximized product backstock on the floor, allowing the second-floor area previously designated for backstock to be used for selling. The design opened 20 percent of the upper floor to create selling and interactive play areas visible from both levels.

Design: Mansour Design, New York City – James Mansour, president; Martin Jerry, vice president of design; William Koo, director of visual merchandising; Manon Zinzell, project manager E.L.C. Team: Early Learning Centre, Swindon, England – Ian Duncan, chief executive; Andrew Crankshaw, managing director; Richard Taylor, retail design controller; John Goddard, property director; Dave Downer, regional manager Fixturing: Ruppel GmbH, Lauda-Konigshofen, Germany Furniture: Ruppel GmbH, Lauda-Konigshofen, Germany Flooring: Amtico International Inc, Coventry, England Ceiling: Armstrong World Industries, Lancaster, Pa. Lighting: Microlights Limited, Wiltshire, England Signage: John Anthony Signs Ltd., Essex, England 3D Characters/Sculpture: Farmer Studios, Leicester, England Shopfront/Store fit: Oakwood Shopfitting, Hants, England Specialist Finishes/Artwork: Rob Sherwood, Rowley Regis, England Structural Engineers: Cameron Taylor Bedford, West Midlands, England

Photography by Jon Arnold, Leichestershire, England

STROUDS HOME COMPASS

IRVINE, CALIF.

In doubling the size of the typical Strouds chain store to 50,000 square feet and in-creasing the product line from bed and bath products to a full line of home furnishings, Strouds Home Compass assumed a new identity. Custom frame display fixtures float in the home decor departments, providing flexible merchandising opportunities and focal dividers for each lifestyle decor. Columns are clad in a brick veneer to add to the warehouse look, while a warm color palette provides a neutral backdrop for each of the lifestyle settings. Natural concrete-colored Marmoleum flooring guides shoppers along the store's circular path. Large transparent graphics suspend- ed from the ceiling help identify departments, where similar merchandise is displayed according to lifestyle rather than brand. Sisal-like natural carpet within depart- ments helps differentiate between product categories and lifestyle vignettes. Changes in type, height and level of light- ing reinforce the ambiance of each home style area. Over- sized window-like lighting fix- tures offer grand-scaled architectural elements to the space.

Design: Jon Greenberg & Associates, Southfield, Mich. – Ken Nisch, chair; Julie Sabourin, account executive; Michael Curtis, creative director; Tony Camilletti, vice president of visual communications; Brian Hurttienne, project manager; Renae Hawley and Jennifer Kaipio, interior designers; Brian Eastman, graphic design director; Val Fischione, graphic designer Strouds Team: Wayne Selness, president; Paul Stenbo, vice president of creative services Architect: LPA, San Diego Lighting Consultant: John Saparano, Lighting Management Inc, New York City General Contractor: Retail Construction Services, Inc. Fixturing: Bon-Art International, Newark, N.J.; California Display, Newark, N.J. Flooring: Marmorette-Gerbert LTD, Lancaster, Pa.; Genuwood-Permagrain Products, Media, Pa.; Atlas Manufacturers, City of Commerce, Calif. Sound System: Bose, BTV Systems, Weeki Wachee, Fla. Concrete Counter Tops: Buddy Rhodes Studio, San Francisco Brick Columns: Scenery West, Hollywood, Calif. White Glass: Krinklglas by Dimensional Plastic Corp., Hialeah, Fla. Metal Mesh: McNichols Co., Tampa, Fla.

Photography by Laszlo Regos, Berkley, Mich.

WILLIAMS-SONOMA

BROADWAY, NEW YORK CITY

Williams-Sonoma's Grande Cuisine concept is intended to continue the company's tradition of "serving serious cooks." This 15,000-square-foot new storefront was designed to respond both to the nineteenth-century light industrial character of the neighborhood and the ornate facades of adjacent buildings. An open store plan highlights the Corinthian columns of the existing interior, with mechanical systems located primarily in perimeter soffits above fixtures to maintain the 19-foot height of the ceiling. Many other prototypical elements of Williams-Sonoma stores, including the Food Hall and differentiated category shops, took new forms in this space, framed by the store's replastered Corinthian columns.

Design: McCall Design Group, San Francisco — Mike McCall, principal; Ken Moy, associate; John Chan, senior project architect; Sing Yip, project architect Williams-Sonoma team: Bud Cope, director of store planning; Richard Altuna, Los Angeles Architect: McCall Design Group, San Francisco General contractor: Fisher Development, Inc., San Francisco Fixturing: Environments, Minnetonka, Minn. Lighting: American Wholesale Lighting, Fremont, Calif. Signage: Thomas Swan Signs, San Francisco

Photography by Andrew Bordwin, New York City

POTTERY BARN

SOHO, NEW YORK CITY

The New York City flagship for Pottery Barn is located in one of SoHo's cast-iron buildings with original storefront, tin ceiling and cast-iron columns. Working with the Landmarks Preservation Board, the designers restored the exterior storefront and painted the building an historically appropriate color that is also in the family of colors characteristic of recent Pottery Barn units. Divided into four zones, the 7,000-square-foot store contains a grand lobby, seasonal shop, design studio and tabletop shop. The design table that traditionally anchors the store is here aligned with the row of columns, linking the design studio to the rest of the space. Original windows (opening onto a light well) were also restored to help create evocative residential-style settings.

Design: Backen Arrigoni & Ross Inc., San Francisco — Howard J. Backen, principal in charge; Hans Baldauf, project manager and senior designer; Ken Jung; Charles Theobald, Susan Gunther, Tim Chappelle, Tim Wong, project team Williams-Sonoma Team: Richard Altuna, Los Angeles Architect: Backen Arrigoni & Ross Inc. Fixturing: Environments, Minnetonka, Minn. Furniture: Denning Cabinetry, San Francisco Signage/graphics: Thomas Swan, San Francisco

Photography by Douglas Dun, San Francisco

AKRIS

BOSTON

Behind a traditional brick and masonry facade is the AKRIS boutique's signature Swiss line of clothing and accessories. The store's interior design theme is based on the relationship between American Federal-style neoclassicism and European Modern design. The wall surfaces and ceiling coves of polished, natural raw-white plaster with subtle variations in tone feature simple geometries and clean white lines. Colorfully upholstered velour sofas and chairs warm the space and soffits above merchandising bays accommodate both backlighting and accent lighting systems focused to emphasize the clothing's fabrics and construction. A bowed wood feature wall of quarter-sawed sycamore contrasts with the white perimeter, while satin-finished oak strip flooring gives the space solidity. Chrome hardware components allow for merchandising flexibility.

Design: Sopha Sa Architects, Paris – Christian Duval and Michel Jambon, architects Bergmeyer Associates, Boston – David Tubridy, AIA, president; Joseph Nevin, principal-in-charge; Joseph Zelloe, AIA, project manager AKRIS Team: AKRIS, St. Gallen, Switzerland – Albert Kriemler, owner and designer; Peter Kriemler, owner; Francesca Laurenzi, director of North American operations; Ellen Gradwahl, boutique manager Architects: Sopha Sa Architects, Paris; Bergmeyer Associates, Boston General Contractor: Shawmut Design and Construction, Boston Fixturing: Mark Ritchey Woodwork, Essex, Mass. Lighting: Johnson Schwinghammer Lighting Consultants Inc., New York City Signage: Signs O' Life, Boston MEP Engineer: The Zade Company, Boston Millwork: Mark Ritchey Woodwork, Essex, Mass.

Photography by Lucy Chen, Somerville, Mass.

RUNNERS' CHOICE

COMMERCE COURT, TORONTO

Relocating into Toronto's business district marked the high-tech running equipment retailer's departure from the mainstream sporting goods approach. Made up of interlocking circular departments and boutiques organized around a central information/meeting area, fixtures in the 5,000-square-foot space have round and oval wood bases and incorporate a system of perforated metal panels. Neutral colors represent the urban running environment, accented by natural blues and greens. Blue neon uplighting give the impression of a city sky; merchandise is lighted by incandescents to best present true colors. Concrete flooring provides a testing ground for running shoes, with vinyl maple wood flooring for indoor shoes.

Design: The International Design Group, Toronto — R. MacLachlan, managing director; Ronald Harris, Jane Nakagawa; Ron Mazereeuw, Andrew Gallici, Grace Eng, Simon Newman, designers General contractor: Premium Plus, Ajax, Ont. Fixturing: Global Store Fixtures, Concord, Ont.; Comatec, Woodbridge, Ont. Flooring: York Marble Tile & Terrazzo, Toronto; Southland Stone, Toronto Lighting: Illuma, Toronto; Juno Lighting, Des Plaines, Ill. Laminates:Octopus Products, Toronto Mannequins/forms: ALU, New York City

Photography by Shin Sugino, Toronto

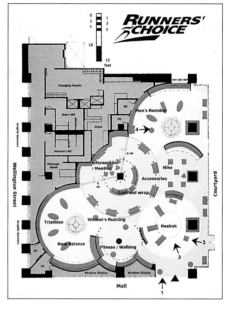

JAEGER

OXFORD, ENGLAND

The first of Jaeger's new international store concepts was positioned to build Jaeger's international credibility and compete in the world designer marketplace. The central entrance of the 2,400-square-foot space is flanked by full-height windows in which pivoting screens of American black walnut can either serve as a backdrop or be used to present merchandise stories on steel hanging rods. Inside, in the women's area, upholstered chairs in taupe suede, French limestone floor, handmade rug and a timber-and-glass table contribute to a feeling of luxurious comfort. Lighting, focused on signature presentations, is directed from coffers. In the formal menswear area, design changes to wood, a dramatic shirt wall and low-level lighting from desk lamps.

Design: 20/20 Design and Strategy Consultants, London — Richard Mott, president; Bernard Dooling, creative director; Simon Stacey and Constantine Lykiardopoulos, project directors; Paul Foley, Sarah Page, designers Jaeger team: Fiona Harris, ceo; Ross Manning, president, Jaeger North America Lighting design: Into Lighting Design Ltd., London General contractor: Charles Barrett Interiors, London Fixturing and interior: Charles Barrett Interiors

Photography by Jon O'Brien, London

VIA SETO

ROSMERE, QUEBEC

The mandate for the Via Seto team was to develop a concept for a men's fashion store in suburban malls, which would cater to men aged 20 to 40 and convey the image of fashionable clothing at affordable prices. Natural stone and a stainless steel sign project the image of "European" fashion, and halogen lighting adds drama and impact. Although symmetrical on plan, the store layout is asymmetrical in its treatment. Stainless steel gives the fitting room and cash areas a high end atmosphere while the color of the fabric and a wood canopy counterbalance the metal with their warmth. Mosaic inserts in the stone floor borrow the colors of the wood and fabric and the shape of the veins in the stone.

Design: Gervais Harding Associés, Montreal – Steve Sutton, principal; Giovanni Bellizzi, project director/designer; James Lee, senior designer Via Seto Team: Tony DelCorpo, owner Lighting Consultants: Futura Industries, Clearfield, Utah Fixturing: J.P. Metal, Montreal Flooring: Murano Ceramics, Montreal Lighting: Juno Lighting, Des Plaines, Ill. Fabrics: Guilford of Maine Textile Resources, Grand Rapids, Mich. Props/decoratives: Les Beaux Ouvrages, Montreal Mannequins/ forms: Seven Continents, Toronto

Photography by Yves Lefebvre, Montreal

XX/XY JEAN STORE

SQUARE ONE SHOPPING CENTER, MISSISSAUGA, ONT.

This new lifestyle jeans concept for the Thrifty's division of Dylex was built around 12 international brands of men's and women's jeans. Design needed to appeal to a young, street-smart customer while respecting the integrity of each brand identity. So the space is organized into tightly focused brand areas, with flexible component wood-and-metal fixturing, ranging from a curved floor-to-ceiling Levi's jeans wall to two-tiered tables and puck wall systems in Pepe Jeans providing a coherent visual identity. Bold graphics programs and custom lighting fixtures contribute to individual brand identities.

Design: Yabu Pushelberg, Toronto — George Yabu, Glenn Pushelberg, Tara Browne, Janis Chow, Chiristina Gustavs, Tracy Morgulis, Mehari Seare, Anthony Tey Thrifty's team: Mickey Maklin, president; Pat Callaghan Graphic design: Boom Design, Toronto Fixturing/furniture: Louis Interiors, Toronto Flooring: Elte Carpets, Toronto Lighting: Capri Lighting, Los Angeles Fabrics: TriTex Marketing, Toronto Signage/graphics: Photoimaging Techniques, Markham, Ont. Mannequins/forms: ALU, New York City

Photography by Robert Burley, Design Archive, Toronto

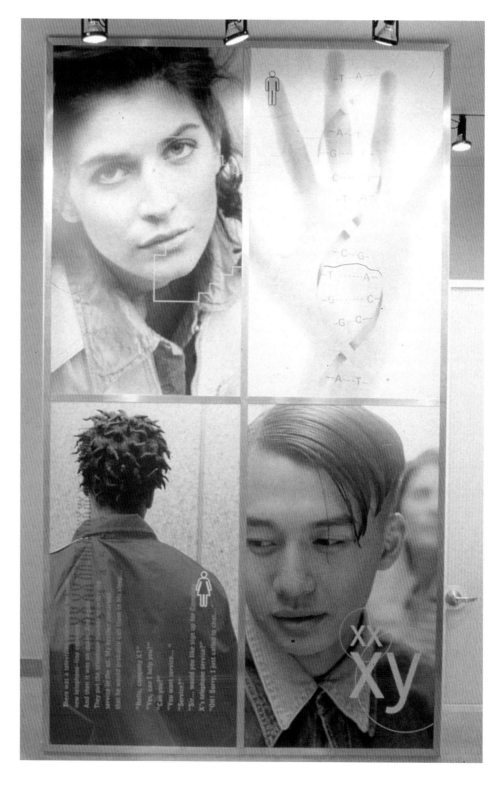

SPECIALTY STORE UNDER 5,000 SQ. FT. FOR SOFTLINES

SAKS FIFTH AVENUE

CHARLESTON, S.C.

Organized around a grand interior court, the new 30,000-square-foot specialty store features alcoves of merchandise to create a residential environment. In the center court, stepped ceiling architecture combines with a perimeter light cove, marble-accented lime floor tiles and specially glazed columns to create a grand space. For a formal, yet comfortable, environment, furnishings include residential-style chairs and tables in a variety of shapes, materials and leg styles. Casework and built-in cabinetry are rich wood tones and brightly lit.

Design: Tucci Segrete & Rosen Consultants, Inc., New York City — Dominick L. Segrete, ceo; Stephen B. Joseph, executive vice president and account director; Edward Calabrese, senior vice president and design director; Mark Orlando, project manager; Vincent D'Armetta, director of production Saks team: Alexandra Notaras, AIA, vice president; Patrick Annello, planner Architect: The Beach Co., Charleston, S.C. Lighting design: Fixturing: Store Fixtures Inc., Ft. Worth, Texas; Vira Mfg., Rahway, N.J. Flooring: Innovative Marble & Tile, Farmindale, N.Y.; Lotus Carpets, Columbus, Ga.; Atlas Carpet, City of Commerce, Calif.; American Olean, Lansdale, Pa. Laminates: Formica, Cincinnati; Laminart, Elk Grove Village, Ill.; Wilsonart, Temple, Texas Wall coverings: Innovations in Wallcoverings, New York City; Genon, Hackensack, N.J.; MDC Wallcoverings, Elk Grove Village, Ill. Fabrics: Design Tex, Woodside, N.Y.; Clarence House, New York City; Brunschwig & Fils, New York City; Jack Lenor Larsen, New York City

Photography by Dub Rogers, New York City

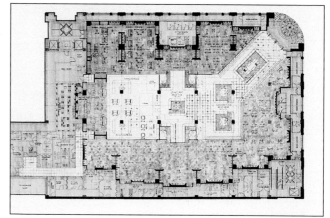

SPECIALTY STORE OVER 5,000 SQ. FT. FOR SOFTLINES

BANANA REPUBLIC

MIAMI BEACH, FLA.

For this two-story store in South Miami Beach's Collins Avenue Art Deco Historic District, Gap designers restored the exterior to its original plan, with the many windows characteristic of a 1928 apartment building. In the 10,162-square-foot interior, art deco elements include antique tables and chairs, two-story columns with silver banded detailing, draped fabric at the fitting room entrance and terrazzo flooring with a custom mosaic pattern. Curving, fluid ceiling lines lead to an oculus open to the floor and skylight above. Lighting is recessed in order not to interrupt these ceiling planes. Custom display fixtures complement the streamlined aluminum railings in the space, while built-in modular cabinets are similar to those in other Banana Republic stores. Along the curving terrazzo stairway is a 40-foot long mural, 20 feet high, commissioned for the project.

Design: Gap Inc. corporate architecture department, San Francisco — Dan Worden, vice president, store design; Mark Koch, director; Erik Tokstad, designer; Tom Pantazis, project manager; Jeff Stitt, architect Lighting design: Grenald Associates, Narbeth, Pa. General contractor: Fisher Development, Inc., San Francisco Mural: Andrew Reid, Miami

Photography by John Dolan, New York City

SPECIALTY STORE OVER 5,000 SQ. FT. FOR SOFTLINES

DFS GALLERIA AT CUSTOMHOUSE

CUSTOM & ALBERT STREETS, AUCKLAND, NEW ZEALAND

The design team faced a unique challenge when refurbishing the landmark Customhouse building, which was built in 1889. The stringent guidelines of the Historic Places Trust stated that nothing could be permanently affixed to either the walls or the ornamental plaster ceiling, so a system of freestanding perimeter fixtures was created for use in the Heritage rooms. Custom carpet runners were designed to protect the original, restored New Zealand Kauri wood plank flooring in the main corridors to the individual vendor boutiques. An atrium situated around the escalator allows daylight and visual access to all of the floors and directs the main flow of traffic through the store. Floors are identified with decorative banners inspired by New Zealand Maori patterns.

Design: Charles Sparks + Company, Westchester, Ill. – Charles Sparks, president, principal-in-charge, designer; Mark McKinney, project manager; Don Stone, lighting designer; Fred Wiedenbeck, color, project, materials designer; Stephanie Arakawa Moore, graphics   DFS Team: Howard Meitiner and Julian Levy, principals; David Charles and Karen Taylor, project development; Greg Trezise, construction manager; Kirsten Sutton, visual merchandising Architect: Peddle Thorp, Auckland   General Contractor: Federal, Auckland   Fixturing: Allen & Chapman, Auckland; Shears & Mack, Auckland   Floor Covering: Masland Carpets Inc, Mobile, Ala.; Interface Floor Coverings, La Grange, Ga.; Edward Fields Custom Carpets, New York City; Jacobsens Creative Surfaces; Tiles Plus; Trethewey Marble & Granite; Tile Warehouse; Forbo Industries Inc, Hazleton, Pa.   Textiles: Glant, Seattle; Gilford Wallcoverings Inc, Jeffersonville, Ind.; Robert Allen Fabrics; Donghia, New York City   Furniture: Goodman Charlton, Los Angeles; Shelby Williams, Morristown, Tenn.; Richard Winter; Donghia, New York City; Niedermaier, Chicago   Custom Light Fittings: Newmetal Crafts   Paint Finishes: Benjamin Moore & Co. Ltd., Montvale, N.J.; Levine & Co. Ltd.; Resene Paints Ltd.   Decorative Murals: Apropos, Minneapolis, Minn.   Laminates: Formica Corporation, Cincinnati Signage: Neo-Neon

Photography by Patrick Reynolds, Auckland, New Zealand

SPECIALTY STORE OVER 5,000 SQ. FT. FOR SOFTLINES

75

EDDIE BAUER

NORTH MICHIGAN AVENUE, CHICAGO

A more refined version of Eddie Bauer's previous flagships, the new 28,500-square-foot Chicago store translates the retailer's rugged, outdoorsy image to a more sophisticated, urban setting. Light coves have been added, fixtures have been updated with a more open design and lighter wood and flooring is now stained concrete instead of tile. Wood plank ceilings, column treatments and massive chandeliers are reminiscent of an upscale hunting lodge. A separate identity for the EBTEK shop housing high-performance sports apparel was created with a distinctive, brightly lit, aluminum logo. In the dramatic 50-foot-high rotunda, visible from both the street and from the retailer's 600-square-foot coffee shop, are a rotating aluminum hanging globe sculpture, symbolizing the world of Eddie Bauer, and the retailer's signature canoes, strapped to the side walls.

Design: FRCH Design Worldwide, Cincinnati — Kevin Roche, Barb Fabing, Tom Horwitz, Tony Nasser, Jay Kratz, Bill Benton, Dave Curtsinger Eddie Bauer team: Bill McDermid, divisional vice president of store development; Mike Miller, director of store design; Kevin Gysler, director of store development; Joe Scheiner, project manager, construction; Jane McCartin, manager of purchasing; Frank Kennard, divisional vice president of visual presentation; Joe Stoneburner, director of visual presentation; Bill Johnston, manager of visual operations Architect: Shaw & Associates, Chicago Lighting: Charles Loomis, Kirkland, Wash. (custom fixtures); Villa Lighting, St. Louis; Brass Light Gallery, Milwaukee Signage/ graphics: Turner Exhibits, Edmonds, Wash. (custom signs); Color 2000, San Francisco (lighted graphics); Image National, Boise, Idaho (storefront signage); Precis Architectural, Kirkland, Wash. (interior signage); Messenger Signs, Seattle (interior signs) Ceiling: Sepia Interior Supply, Seattle (tile and grid) Millwork/fixtures: Amstore Corp., Muskegon, Mich.; Eurotek Store Fixtures, Kent, Wash.; J.R. Abbott Construction, Seattle; Synsor Corp., Woodinville, Wash.; Russell William Ltd., Odenton, Md.; Omaha Fixtures, Omaha, Neb. Flooring: Bomanite, Madera, Calif. (concrete); CSM Inc., Woodinville, Wash. (stained concrete); Buell Hardwood Floors, Dallas (wood) Props/decoratives: Can Am Trading, Greenfield, Mass.; Golden Oldies, Flushing, N.Y.

Photography by Paul Bielenberg, Los Angeles

SPECIALTY STORE OVER 5,000 SQ. FT. FOR SOFTLINES

SAKS FIFTH AVENUE

HOUSTON GALLERIA, HOUSTON

Housed in the former Marshall Field's store, Saks sought a new image that would offer a level of luxury and resources to their customers that would be Saks' own. The atrium, the key signature piece, is a three-story-high space where the architecture of the building interior is established. A sense of classic proportions and fine materials underscore the look. Faux limestone pilasters, bronze and nickel railings and silver leaf accents set the tone. The limestone architecture, accentuated with cherry wood, is recalled on shopfronts and unifying facades.

Design: Tucci, Segrete & Rosen Consultants, Inc., New York City – Dominick Segrete, AIA, ISP, president; Stephen Joseph, executive vice president; Edward Calabrese, senior vice president/creative director; Lisa Contreras, vice president/creative resources; Santo Zappala, vice president, director of production; Danny Dong, project manager Saks Team: Wayne Hussey, senior vice president, real estate/planning/design and visual; Randy Ridless, vice president, store planning and design; Alexandra Notaras, AIA, vice president, construction; Errol Pierre, store planner; Walt Lichtenberg, director of construction - western region. Architects: Philip Johnson, New York City (original building facade); Morris Architects, Houston (local architect for remodel) General Contractor: Pepper Lawson Construction Inc., Katy, Texas Fixturing: Oklahoma Fixture Company, Tulsa, Okla.; Edron Fixture Corporation, Miami; Abbey Store Fixtures Ltd., Markham, Ont. Faux Finishes: Evergreen Studios, New York City Wall coverings: Anya Larkin, New York City; Brunschwig & Fils, New York City; Elizabeth Dow, New York City Flooring: Innovative Marble & Tile, Hauppauge, N.Y.; Atlas Carpet, Los Angeles; Bloomsburg Carpet, New York City; Stark Carpet, New York City

Photography by Dub Rogers, New York City

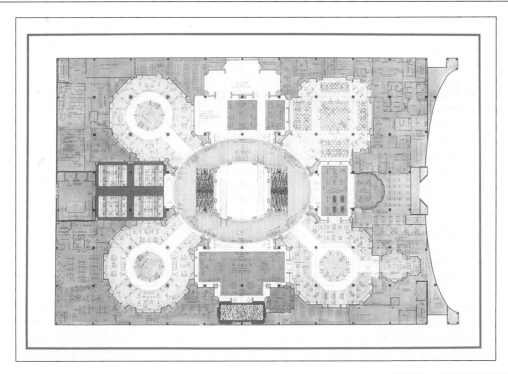

REI FLAGSHIP STORE

SEATTLE

A 65-foot tall climbing "pinnacle" overshadows the climbing department of the new REI (Recreational Equipment Inc.) flagship. The store's 80,000-square-foot interior reflects the "honest rusticity" of the REI mission and incorporates as many natural and recycled materials as possible. The lobby-like entrance sets the tone, with a large information desk made of wood slabs perched on rock pedestals, racks of travel brochures for the Pacific Northwest and an archival display that focuses on the company's heritage, philosophies and the adventures of its members. The entrance also provides a striking view of the climbing pinnacle.

Architecture, materials and fixtures reflect the beauty of the outdoors: blond wood, honey-colored sandstone, matte-gray metals and lots of windows. Much of the first story is open through to the roof, creating an expansive, light-filled atrium. The first floor two-story sandstone fireplace reinforces the lodge-like setting.

Architecture/design: Mithun Partners Inc., Seattle (consulting architect) — Thomas Emrich AIA, president/project manager; Bert Gregory AIA, partner in charge of design; Robert Deering AIA, project architect; Hao (Casey) Huang and Ken Boyd, architects REI design team: Wally Smith, president; Jerry Chevassus, director of retail; Terri Perlman, merchandising project manager; Elaine Jorgenson, merchandise presentation coordinator Environmental Graphic Design: The Leonhardt Group, Seattle — Ted Leonhardt, president; Mark Popich, lead designer; Lori Kent, project manager; Corbin Design, Traverse City, Mich. — Jim Harper, Robert Brengman and Heath Gnopper, design team Credits continued on p.173.

Photography by Robert Pisano, Seattle

LARGE-FORMAT SPECIALTY (NON-DISCOUNT) STORE OVER 30,000 SQ. FT.

83

LARGE-FORMAT SPECIALTY (NON-DISCOUNT) STORE OVER 30,000 SQ. FT.

FAO SCHWARZ

THE FORUM SHOPS OF CAESAR'S PALACE, LAS VEGAS

A fully animated Trojan Horse over four stories high greets shoppers as they enter the mall plaza. The "ultimate pull-toy" nods his head in greeting as his mane strobes with colored light, his eyes blink and his nostrils blow smoke. The horse appears to be rolling into the atrium from the arched entry to the store. Animatronic characters populate the horse, appearing from behind trap doors in his sides and belly. Customers can travel through a dinosaur rib cage to an interactive shop styled after "The Lost World," sit at large dice tables beneath stacks of money in the "Monopoly Coffee Bar," or enjoy intergalactic juice drinks at the "Star Wars Cantina Bar." In the Star Wars shop, authentic scale replicas of Star Wars spacecraft suspended below the ceiling en-gage in a laser battle, while the "Millennium Falcon Cockpit" provides a multi-screen audio-visual experience.

Design: J. Newbold Associates, Inc., New York City – Joanne Newbold, principal and designer; Laurence Koplick, Jeanne Ferlesch, George Ladas and Sharon Pachter, designers; John Kehe, graphic design FAO Schwarz Team: John Eyler, chair and ceo; Dik Glass, vice president of store development; John Thaxton, senior project manager; Tom Crossman, director of visual display Architect: Associates in Architecture and Design, Scottsdale, Ariz. Lighting consultants: Johnson Schwinghammer Lighting Consultants, Inc., New York City General Contractor: FAO Schwarz Store Development, New York City Fixtures: Associated Wood Products, San Diego; Woodmasters Design and Manufacturing, Addison, Ill.; Pinehurst Woodworking Co. Inc.; Gore Manufacturing, N. Charleston, S.C.; Theme Tech, Phoenix; HED Food Service, Rocky Mount, N.C. Flooring: Amtico International Inc, Atlanta, Ga.; Arcon Architectural Concrete, Las Vegas; Durkan Patterned Carpet, Dalton, Ga. Ceiling: Chicago Metallic, Chicago Lighting: High End Systems Inc, Austin, Texas; Contech, Elk Grove Village, Ill.; Lithonia, Conyers, Ga.; Mid-West Chandelier Co., Kansas City, Kansas; Halo Lighting Brand Cooper Lighting, Elk Grove Village, Ill.; Lightolier, Fall River, Mass.; Donovan Design, Southampton, N.Y. Laminates: Formica Corporation, Cincinnati Signage: Fiber Optic Systems Inc., Whitehouse Station, N.J.; Andre's Imaging, Chicago Props/decoratives/theming: The Larson Company, Tucson, Ariz.; Garner Holt Productions, San Bernardino, Calif.; Florida Entech Corp., Winter Park, Fla.; Theme Tech, Phoenix; Penwal, Rancho Cucamonga, Calif.; Fibervision, Tucson, Ariz.; Rathe Productions, New York City; Advanced Animation, Stockbridge, Vt.; Crespinel Studio, Seattle

Photography by Peter Paige Photography, Harrington Park, N.J.

LARGE-FORMAT SPECIALTY (NON-DISCOUNT) STORE OVER 30,000 SQ. FT.

87

LARGE-FORMAT SPECIALTY (NON-DISCOUNT) STORE OVER 30,000 SQ. FT.

89

M&M'S WORLD

SHOWCASE MALL, LAS VEGAS

The design team wished to reposition the brand, product and packaging of Ethel M Chocolates to create a strong, memorable and category-differentiating identity. Their challenge was to plan a four-floor glass-fronted store with only vertical transportation. The M&M's World combines nearly 26,000 square feet of retail area on four floors. From the exterior, a large-scale M&M's bag appears to spill across the glass curtain wall. Focal merchandising fixtures are located at the entry of each floor. On the first floor, a focal fixture topped by a giant cupid invites customers to customize boxes of their personal favorites from the Ethel M Chocolates collection. Floor two houses a 12-foot "Colorworks" fixture that dispenses from a range of 14 different M&M's colors, and the fourth floor features a huge M&M's bag that appears to spill peanut M&M's onto the cashwrap. Signage and graphics incorporate cupids and shots of classic movie kisses to capitalize on the romance of chocolate.

Design: The Retail Group, Seattle – J'Amy Owens, president, principal-in-charge; Cristopher Gunter, ceo, principal-in-charge; Cara McClarty and Rob Coburn, project managers; Anne Croney and Greg Arhart, co-creative directors; Karyn Leemans, Conrad Chin, David Kelly and Greg Moore, store planning; Eunice Chan, graphics and signage, packaging and logo; Casey Cram, graphics and signage; Ashley Bogle, packaging and logo Architects: Cunningham Group, Solberg + Lowe, Marina Del Rey, Calif. Lighting Consultants: Joe Kaplan Archtiectural Lighting, Los Angeles; Landmark Entertainment Group, N. Hollywood, Calif.

Photography by Craig Harrold, Seattle

LARGE-FORMAT SPECIALTY STORE OVER 30,000 SQ. FT.

VIACOM ENTERTAINMENT STORE
CHICAGO

The store provides an immersive entertainment shopping experience that offers consumers a direct connection to six of the company's most popular brands while reinforcing Viacom's corporate identity. The entrance features a computerized light show of brand logos and images, and an electronic store directory in the form of six monitors. The store's dynamic architectural design, with its high ceilings, exposed ductwork and wide-open selling areas, is immediately visible. Each brand area has its own unique style and design elements. The Nick at Nite area, for example, features retro-contempo styling and vintage TV sculpture, an "I Love Lucy" diorama, a "Happy Days" jukebox and a cashwrap designed like a fifties kitchen. The Star Trek environment features full-scale aliens and a transport area where customers can take home a photo of themselves being "beamed up." A touch-screen console similar to those used on the Enterprise accesses ship information. Overlooking the rotunda from the second floor, the Station Break Cafe is a 70-seat restaurant with a 10-foot stage used for guest appearances and live entertainment.

Design: FRCH Design Worldwide, Cincinnati — concept design of Paramount and Star Trek — Barbara Fabing, design principal; Tom Horowitz, project principal Pompei A.D., New York City — concept design of MTV and Nick at Nite Fitch, Columbus, Ohio — concept design, Nickelodeon and MTV shops Viacom Retail Group, Store Development, Dallas — Lori Wegman, vice president of store development; Robert Anthony, director of media technology; Brian Cornelius, director of store development; Eric Corti, director of construction management; Mary Martel, manager of visual merchandise; Jane McNeely, director of graphics and scenic design Architect: FRCH Design Worldwide, Cincinnati Media Technology Consultant: Edwards Technology, El Segundo, Calif. MEP Engineers: ADG, St. Louis General Contractor: Capitol Construction, Wheeling, Ill. Flooring: Arrow Patterned Concrete, Bloomington, Ill. (concrete floor staining) Fixturing: FHC, Chicago; Design Fabricators, Lafayette, Colo. Signage and Graphics: Engrafix Architectural Signage Inc, St. Louis; Skyline, Chicago; Whiteway Signs, Chicago; X Design, Columbus, Ohio Scenic Design: Joel Klaff, Chicago; Nick Studios, Orlando; TW Design, Houston Media Technology: Eastman Kodak, Rochester, N.Y.; Muze, New York City

Photography by Dan Forer, Miami

SPORTMART

LOMBARD, ILL.

Distinguished in the sporting goods industry by its signature groupings of hardgoods and softgoods together into four worlds of sports, Sportmart is organized around a central concourse feature area. Suit Up (team sports), Lace Up (footwear), Burn It (workout) and Get Out (outdoors and camping) each are identified by huge graphic "billboards" and vertical pylons identified with the name of the section. Flooring throughout the store range from industrial diamond plate stainless steel in the concourse to hardwood in the basketball shop, rubber matting in workout, sisal carpeting in the golf club area and vinyl in footwear. Interactive elements include a "how high can you jump" pylon, virtual reality hole for golfing and swing analyzing station, educational in-line skating videos and a basketball court area.

Design: Schafer Associates, Inc., Oakbrook Terrace, Ill. — Robert W. Schafer, chair and ceo; Beth Howley, project director; R.H. Lubben, project planner; Jeff Stompor, project designer; Lisa Sallwasser, senior graphic designer; Rob Soderholm, project manager; Walter Plavsic, job captain; Andrea Schindlebeck, graphic designer Sportmart team: Mark Scott, president; Rob Morrison, vice president Marts; John Lowenstein, vice president operations; Jim Conroy, vice president of construction; Harry Hunter, director construction; Jeff Olson, director of visual merchandising Outside consultant: Adrienne Weiss Corp., Los Angeles (graphics, illustrations, packaging, signing, displays, promotional concepts and private label product development) Architect: Ridgeland Associates, Oakbrook Terrace, Ill. Signage/graphics design: Adrienne Weiss Corp., Los Angeles, in collaboration with Schafer Associates General contractor: Osman Construction, Arlington Heights, Ill. Fixturing: Nu-Era, St. Louis; Spectrum, Freeport, N.Y.; Lozier, Omaha, Neb.; Ontario Store Fixtures, Weston, Ont. Flooring: Harbinger, Atlanta; Lees, Greensboro, N.C.; Nora Rubber Flooring, Highland Park, Ill.; Armstrong, Lancaster, Pa.; Tajima, Arlington Heights, Ill.; Forbo, Hazleton, Pa. Lighting: Indy Lighting, Indianapolis Wall coverings: Marlite, Dover, Ohio; Sherwin Williams, Cleveland (paint); Benjamin Moore, Montvale, N.J. (paint)   Materials/finishes: Wilsonart, Temple, Texas (laminates); Mercer, Woodale, Ill. (vinyl); Formica, Cincinnati (metal finishes); Joseph T. Ryerson, Chicago (metal finishes); Stylmark, Minneapolis (metal finishes); Cres Light, Chicago (metal finishes); Resolite, Pittsburgh (corrugated plastic) Signage: Andres Imaging and Graphics, Chicago; 3M Commercial Graphics, St. Paul, Minn.; Clear Corp., Minnetonka, Minn.; Eddy Associates, New Berlin, Wis. Sound effects: AEI, Seattle

Photography by Bob Briskey, Briskey Photography, Hinsdale, Ill.

BARRY KIESELSTEIN-CORD

PALM BEACH, FLA.

The first freestanding U.S. store for this the designer of jewelry, handbags, belts and luxury accessories, consists of a carved limestone entry portal, a foyer and subtly separate sales areas for jewelry and leather goods. Influenced by art deco furniture, the entire store interior is based on curves. Serpentine floor-to-ceiling walls of mahogany paneling echo the jewelry forms. Other features include custom dyed suede wall, custom-dyed carpet, thirties-designed club chairs, hand-carved store logo and gently curved quarter-vision jewelry cases.

Design: Christopher Barriscale Architects, New York City — Christopher Barriscale, principal; Don Lee, project architect; C. Warnick, M. Sprug, designers Client team: Hattie Whitehead, fashion director Architect: Christopher Barriscale Architects Lighting design: Thomas Thompson Lighting Design, New York City General contractor: Fisher Clark, W. Palm Beach, Fla. Fixturing: Rogers & Rogers Inc., New York City Furniture: Poltrona Frau, New York City (club chairs) Flooring: Beauvais Carpets, New York City (custom carpet)

Photography by Ross Muir, New York City

PATRONIK DESIGNS JEWELRY GALLERY

BURLINGAME, CALIF.

Housing both the jeweler's workshop/studio and his work, this 900-square-foot gallery is an amalgamation of three of the jeweler's images of his space. The overall framework is that of the white-box gallery with wood floor; within that, the reliquary wall on the right side of the store leans in like a cave wall and refers to the ancient catacombs and reliquaries where precious items were stored. In addition, the idea of the contemporary industrial workshop is communicated through the jeweler's work space in the back of the store, clad in galvanized and copper siding. Suspended light fixtures in this area were designed for the space by a local artisan. Tying the project together is the jewelry, which is presented on copper pedestals, in shadowboxes and in custom fixtures in the reliquary wall niches.

Design: Miroglio Architecture + Design, Joel Miroglio, designer Patronik team: Nick and Christine Kosturos, owners
Architect: Miroglio Architecture + Design General contractor: Greco Petersen Construction, Burlingame, Calif. Fixturing:
Magic Glass Fine Showcases, San Francisco Flooring: Harris-Tarkett, Johnson City, Tenn. Lighting: Neidhardt
Production, Redwood City, Calif. Laminates: Abet Laminati, Teterboro, N.J. Signage/graphics: A Better Image Sign
Co., Castro Valley, Calif.

Photography by Heidi Grassley, Oakland, Calif.

FRUITS & PASSION

GALERIES D'ANJOU, MONTREAL

The 15-by-17-foot boutique for a line of body and lifestyle products was created in a kiosk structure provided by the shopping center. The space was designed with three openings and mobile display units that could be pulled outside the kiosk for maximum visibility. Design was inspired by Gaugin's work, and large-scale portions of his paintings were printed on plastified canvas to wrap the metal columns of the mall structure, as well as backdrops for mobile and fixed display units. Printed canvas creates a "ceiling" for the kiosk and self-stick tiles were printed with Gaugin imagery to cover the mall's tile flooring. Products are merchandised on glass shelves inside the kiosk, on small tables with adjustable shelves, mobile tables and carts, and on mini-leaf tables. Since its debut, the kiosk concept has also been applied to corporate and franchise in-line boutiques.

Design: Gervais Harding Associes, Montreal — Pierre Richard Robitaille, project director/designer; Sophie Lemarbre, intermediate designer   Client team: Jean Hurteau, owner/president   General contractor: Conception CAMA, Boucherville, P.Q.   Fixturing: Roy Metal, Montreal   Furniture: Ebenisterie Norclaire, Boucherville, P.Q.   Flooring/ceiling/signage/graphics: Deck-Art Grande Impression, Laval, P.Q.   Lighting: Lightolier, Fall River, Mass.

Photography by Yves Lefebvre, Montreal

LYNX GOLF TRADE SHOW ENVIRONMENT
PGA GOLF SHOW, LAS VEGAS

With only a 67-day lead time, the design team was charged with developing a booth to feature a new positioning for the company, including a new logo. The team focused on the spirit of the game of golf, helping visitors connect with the positive emotions evoked by the game. Lengths of the booth's "walls" are made of translucent screening that allows visitors glimpses into the environment. The physical experience of the booth echoes the experience of playing golf: a wooden bridge over a bed of fresh grass carries visitors into the booth, where a gravel floor and the sound of water sprinklers in the distance lend an outdoor feel. Golf clubs are supported and cross-merchandised with Lynx Golf apparel. Designed to be flexible, this first booth measured 50-by-50 feet, but will be expanded to 80-by- 80feet in future installations.

Design: Fitch Inc., Worthington, Ohio — Mark Artus, project manager; Bruce Shepherd and Jacquie Richmond, associate vice presidents; Stuart Hunter, Paul Lycett, Clint Bova and Kathleen Goode, senior associates Lynx Golf Team: David Schaefer, president and ceo; Robert Stenby, vice president of marketing; Denis Zimmerman General Contractor: 12-20, Orlando Fixturing: Novak and Associates, Chicago Furniture: 12-20, Orlando Flooring: 12-20, Orlando Lighting: Lighting Management Inc, New York City Laminates:Nevamar, Odenton, Md. Signage: 12-20, Orlando Graphics:Universal Color, Orlando

Photography by Mark Steele, Fitch Inc., Worthington, Ohio

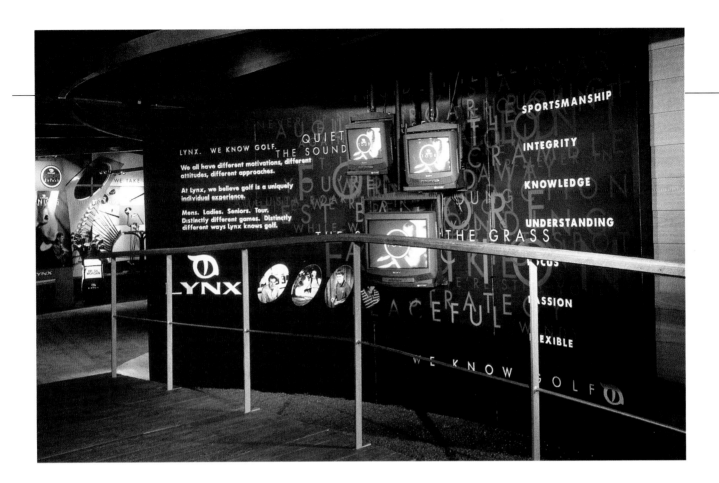

LIQUOR CONTROL BOARD OF ONTARIO

NEW IMAGE STORE DESIGN, TORONTO

The Liquor Control Board of Ontario (LCBO) wanted to rework its typical liquor store design used for the majority of its locations. The challenge was to create a new plan focused on customer service with a lighter, romantic atmosphere. The layout encourages exploration and browsing by weaving through the entire store. A sunny courtyard atmosphere is created with a yellow cream perimeter soffitt with subtly stenciled sage green grapes, vines and hops and accent pin-on signage. Economical track lighting and a 2-by-2-foot T-bar ceiling with color-corrected fluorescent lighting in the general area contribute to a sunlit atmosphere. Above the customer service area is a hand-painted trompe l'oeil arbor of entwined grapes, vines and hops anchored by a custom-designed gray metal chandelier. The interior color scheme consists of sage green, cream, white, natural and pearwood-colored maple, and sand and terra cotta-colored, two-tone linoleum flooring simulates gravel courtyards.

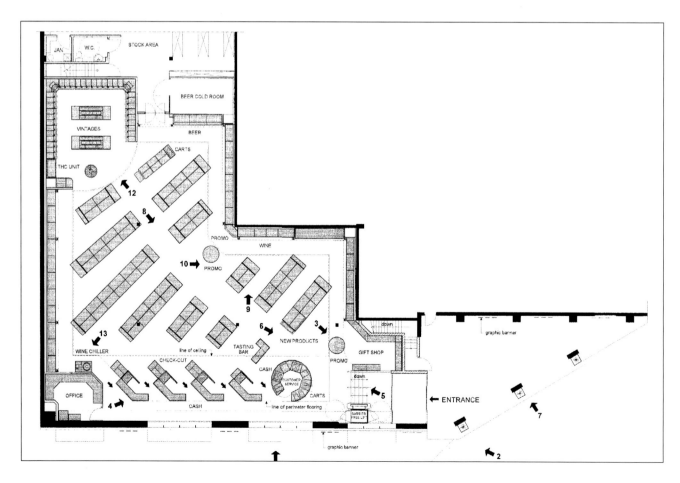

Design: Fiorino Design Inc., Toronto – Nella Fiorino, principal; Miodrag Antic, CAD technician; Vilija Gacionis, interior designer LCBO Team: Jackie Bonic, Nancy Cardinal, Kayla Janjic Architect: Kneider Architects, Toronto General Contractor: Rutherford Contracting Ltd., Gormley, Ont. Fixturing: Hutton's Custom Woodwork Ltd., London, Ont. Flooring: Forbo Industries Inc., Hazleton, Pa. Ceiling: David Adolphus, Highland Creek, Ont. Lighting: Lightolier, Fall River, Mass. Laminates: Nevamar International Paper, Odenton, Md.; Wilsonart International, Temple, Texas Wall Coverings: Sico Paints, Etobicoke, Ont.; Benjamin Moore & Co. Ltd., Montvale, N.J. Signage: Sunset Neon, Burlington, Ont. Graphics: Heather Cooper Co. Ltd., Toronto Props/decoratives: Visions Display Inc., Toronto

LIQUOR CONTROL BOARD OF ONTARIO

MARKET VILLAGE, TORONTO

Targeted toward Chinese immigrants, whose culture uses spirits as status symbols for entertainment and gifts, the government-operated 650-square-foot boutique alludes to an eastern influence in design. Pedimented columns, inspired by ancient Asian portals, frame the entry, and all category signage is bilingual English and Chinese. Modrian-like display cubes comprise the "wall of spirits," while the "power" wall is purple, a color representing wealth, power and respect in Chinese culture. Sensitive to the principles of feng shui, mahogany-colored cherry wood, eggplant purple, spring green and pale yellow make up the color palette.

Design: The International Design Group, Toronto — R. MacLachlan, managing director; David Newman, Donna Lawson, Andrew Gallici, Josee De Luca Seston LCBO team: Jackie Bonic, Noah Shopsowitz, Nancy Cardinal General contractor/fixturing: Salwood General Contractors, Mississauga, Ont. Flooring: Forbo Industries, Hazelton, Pa. Lighting: Juno Lighting, Des Plaines, Ill. Laminates: Nevamar, Odenton, Md.

Photography: Robert Burley, Design Archives, Toronto

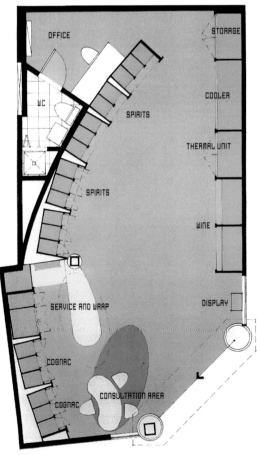

LIQUOR CONTROL BOARD OF ONTARIO

MANULIFE CENTER, TORONTO

In expanding a 3,000-square-foot space to 4,500 square feet, this government-operated store was intended to offer customers information about alcohol and food and ways to combine them. The design firm chose to emphasize the romantic origins of the products through color, texture and art, primarily drawn from the south of France and northern Italy. The sunny, courtyard atmosphere includes yellow/cream stuccoed perimeter curved walls, sand- and terracotta-colored linoleum, cream tongue-and-groove paneling and maple fixtures with cream-colored laminate shelving. To eliminate the customary barrier of check-out counters, the circular information station is centered under a hand-painted arbor of grapes, vines and hops, with cashwraps fanning out to one side of the entrance.

Design: Fiorino Design Inc., Toronto — Nella Fiorino, principal; Vilija Gacionis, Wendy Hung, Miodrag Antic, Jennifer Trabert, Annie Chan LCBO team: Jackie Bonic and Kayla Janjic, store planning; Nancy Cardinal, marketing Graphic design: Heather Cooper, Toronto Mural: David Adolphus, Toronto Fixturing: Salwood General Contractors, Mississauga, Ont. Flooring: Phoenix Floor, Rexdale, Ont. Lighting: Halo, Elk Grove Village, Ill.; Aquan Creations, Toronto Laminates: Formica, Cincinnati; Nevamar, Odenton, Md.

Photography by Robert Burley, Design Archive, Toronto

LIPTON TEAHOUSE
PASADENA, CALIF.

The Thomas J. Lipton Company, the largest producer of tea in the world, decided to extend its brand into the retail format of a teahouse, with the potential for 200 shops to be built nationwide. The project included not only the architectural design of the prototype store, but the brand identity for the teahouse as well, incorporating Lipton's culture, quality and tradition in the world of tea. The palette is warm and was chosen to reflect the greens of the tea plant and the toasty goldens of the tea beverage. An information rail at the front of the shop engages customers at counter height with images, text and graphics from Lipton's history and tea culture. Light wood, colored glass, upholstered banquettes and evocative images of tea leaves create a soothing environment that helps to recast Lipton's presence in the consumer marketplace.

Design: Donovan and Green, New York City – Nancye Green, project director; Andrew Drews, creative director; Paul Soulellis, project manager; Vanessa Ryan, John Chu and Glennys Anglada, designers Lipton Teahouse Team: Jim Reid, president of Lipton Professional Markets Group; Gabby Ferraro, project director; Peter Goggi, director of tea buying; Rich Collins, vice president of customer management; John Sullivan, vice president of sales and food service; Joe Russo, director Architect: Donovan and Green, New York City General Contractor: GG and M Construction, Inc., Pasadena, Calif. Furniture: Thonet Hoffman, Statesville, N.C. Fabrics: Knoll Textiles, New York City; Maharam, New York City Signage: Coast Sign Inc., Anaheim, Calif.

Photography by Jim Hedrich, Hedrich Blessing Photography, Chicago

BIG BEAR

DUBLIN, OHIO

In positioning Big Bear as the area's market leader in prepared foods/home meal replacement, these departments were located at the front of the store and emphasized through bold photo-realistic graphic elements, island and kiosk-style category fixtures and dramatic lighting. Expansion of non-food merchandise, especially cosmetics, health and beauty care, housewares, pet foods and international products enlarges one-stop shopping convenience. Full-service departments include Blockbuster Video, a bank, drycleaners, pharmacy, floral department, catering consultants, photo developing and garden center. Design elements include teal, fuchsia and purple department signage on black backgrounds, and corrugated metal awnings, wrought iron and vinyl wood planking for a traditional farm market visual appeal.

Design: Programmed Products, Novi, Mich. — Llew Reska, president; John Zafarana, ceo Big Bear team: headed by Steve Breech Architects: Meacham & Apel, Columbus, Ohio (interior); Sullivan & Gray, Columbus, Ohio (exterior) General contractor: Continental Real Estate, Columbus, Ohio Interior design/decor fabrication: Programmed Products Corp., Plymouth, Mich. Flooring: Armstrong World Industries, Lancaster, Pa.; Wonder Works of America, Brooklyn, N.Y.; Dal Tile, Dallas Lighting: Indy Fixtures, Fisher, Ind.; Holophane, Newark, Ohio; Metalux, Americus, Ga. Fixtures: Inglebarr, Inc., Chillicothe, Ohio (custom cabinetry); Fortin Welding, Columbus, Ohio (iron works); Lozier, Omaha, Neb. (sales area shelving); InterMetro Industries, Wilkes-Barre, Pa. (sales area shelving); Hussman, Briedgeton, Mo. (refrigerated cases); Amtekco Industries, Columbus, Ohio (produce tables); Columbus Show Case, Columbus, Ohio (bakery cases) Signage: Ritchey Signs, Zanesville, Ohio (illuminated interior signs); Danite Sign Co., Columbus, Ohio (illuminated exterior signs) Ceiling: Custom Architectural Services, Atlanta (grid beam ceiling)

Photography by Llew M. Reszka, Novi, Mich.

FIERA NOVA

TELHEIRAS, PORTUGAL

Fiera Nova's strategy with this new design was to increase customers' frequency of visits to the food and general merchandise hypermarket. Focused on value-priced and promotional merchandise, the space locates fresh foods and produce along the perimeters, with hardlines and packaged goods at the center or to one side, depending on each real-estate situation. Wide aisles and icon-based graphics are color-coded to aid navigation and a multi-lingual customer base. To add to the open and airy atmosphere, fabric canopies soften architecture and lighting in the fresh foods area.

Design: Retail Planning Associates, Columbus, Ohio — Doug Cheesman, chair; Gerry Postlewaite, account executive; David Martin, project manager; Edd Johns, retail strategist; John Pinder, environmental designer; Mike Sims, planner; Frank Amankwah, merchandiser; Perry Kotik; Andrew Dornan, Russell Holmes, visual communication Fiera Nova team: Francisco Dos Santos, ceo Flooring: Focus Ceramics, Weybridge, U.K. Lighting: Erco Lighting, London Materials: Architen Design Build, Bristol, U.K. Signage/graphics: Electrotech Commerce, London; Sign Specialists, London

MAXI & CIE DISCOUNT SUPERMARKET

BOUCHERVILLE, QUE.

The design objective for this supermarket was to create a discount store that is visually exciting and consistent with the "big box" store image. Effective, economical and unpretentious finishes such as plastic laminate, corrugated metal and galvanized metal were incorporated in strong, appealing color schemes to create a fresh and clean look. To emphasize the discount feel of the store, the design team created an easy to shop "Cartesian" traffic pattern, which encourages the shopper to shop each section at a time. A combination of a large yellow arch, a suspended grid for accent lighting, gooseneck lamps, spiral galvanized columns and bold colors is incorporated to frame the counter space and to create presence in the store. The bank and photo service areas are located off the entrance to allow for convenient access without forcing the customer to penetrate the store area, and the photo development area can be seen from a distance. Free-standing arches in the cosmetics area are given a slightly more upscale feel with wood finish plastic laminate, and suspended ceiling grids support warmer accent lighting and reinforce a more human scale.

Design: Pappas Design Studio Inc., Montreal – Bess Pappas, president; Susan Reed, designer Maxi & CIE Team: Alain Foudreau, planner; Claire Cote, director; Chantal Glenisson, equipment Architect: Gross, Kaplin, Coviensky, Montreal Outside Design Consultants: A 2 Zee Grafix General Contractor: C.A.L. Construction, Montreal Fixturing: Etalex, Montreal; Roll-It, Montreal Furniture: Modul Fab, Quebec City Flooring: Mannington Commercial, Calhoun, Ga. Lighting: Lumitech, Montreal Laminates: Formica Corporation, Cincinnati; Nevamar International Paper, Odenton, Md.; Abet Laminati, Englewood, N.J. Signage: Media Modul, St.-Mathias. Que.

Photography by Yves Lefebvre, Montreal

PCC NATURAL MARKETS
SEATTLE

The 13,000-square-foot Puget Consumers Cooperative is marked on the exterior by a huge graphic panel inspired by roadside stand imagery. Interior emphasis is on the beauty of the produce, bulk beans and grains, herbs and spices, with broad aisles and natural lighting to resemble an open-air market. Produce preparation areas and staff activities, in addition to a deli and juice and espresso bar, are also within the store, adding to the busy public market atmosphere. Design details include earthtone-stained concrete floor, semi-transparent stained MDF casework and custom light fixtures made from colanders and cheese-graters.

Design: NBBJ Retail Concepts, Seattle — James Adams, principal; Craig Hardman, project manager; George Ostrow, architect PCC team: Jeff Voltz, general manager; Lori Ross, store planner Architect: NBBJ Retail Concepts General contractor: The Rafn Co., Kirkland, Wash. Fixturing: Madix, Terrell, Texas (grocery shelving); Northwest Fixtures, Seattle (custom casework) Flooring: CSM, Woodinville, Wash. Lighting: Nemco, Seattle Laminates: Big Bear, Seattle Signage: Trademarx, Seattle

Photography by Paul Warchol, New York City

BENIHANA RESTAURANT

PICCADILLY, LONDON

One of the goals of the new design for Benihana was to provide an exciting background for the culinary theater of tabletop Japanese Hibachi-style cuisine. Located in Piccadilly, the 10,700-square-foot restaurant's fragmented interior and varying floor levels required a circular floor plan that directs patrons to follow a path identified by blue tiles and "floating" skylights. Within the 5,600-square-foot restaurant space, Tepannaki tables combine blond and red woods in the tabletop, with stainless steel hoods above. Elegant ramps, backed with blond wood paneling and backlit, unite two separate dining areas and connect different floor levels.

Design: The International Design Group, Toronto — Ron MacLachlan, managing director; David Newman, Constanza Carsten, Ron Mazereeuw Architect: Carnell Green Partnership, London General contractor: Takenaka (UK) Ltd., London Flooring: Vorwerk, Switzerland (carpet) Laminates: Formica, Italy Fabric: Crayfourds, London (chair upholstery) Artwork: Robert O'Dea, London

Photography by Nik Milner, London

EMERALD PLANET

NEW YORK CITY

Offering a new type of fast food, this "wrap and smoothie" eatery aims to be contemporary and functional. The design vocabulary of the 1,700-square-foot space is based on sage, wheat, olive and ochre painted walls to provide a background for glass, stone and concrete surfaces and natural, olive and aubergine stained cherry wood. For contrast, gun-metal and rebar accents are used on tabletops, stool legs, eat-in counters and the service bar. Zinc meridian strips in the concrete floor curve to match the lines of the banquette and service bar, as well as the placement of pendant light fixtures. Graphics include banners in a natural color palette and a framed collage of natural and multi-ethnic images in the back of the space.

Design: Ronnette Riley Architect, New York City — Ronnette Riley, principal; Norine Bagate, project manager; Roberto Bajandas, Melissa Dymock Architect: Ronnette Riley Architect Graphic design: Lisa Mazur/Esther Bridavsky, New York City Fixturing: Design Fabricators, Cranston, R.I. Furniture: Waldners, New York City Flooring: LM Scofield Co., Douglasville, Ga. Lighting: Lighting Collaborative, New York City Laminates: Abet Laminati, Teterboro, N.J. Signage/ graphics: Kaltech, New York City (bound signs and window decals); Vomela, St. Paul, Minn. (mural); Kraus & Sons, New York City (banners); Stelmark, Vancouver, B.C. (menuboard)

Photography by Dub Rogers, New York City

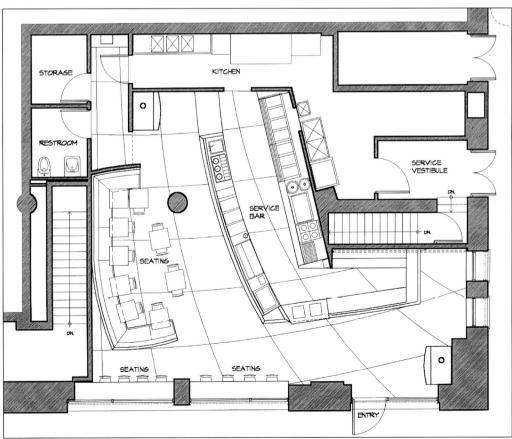

WEST END MARKETPLACE

DALLAS

This third-floor food court in a renovated Texas historic warehouse was designed with a western, urban theme in order to become a destination point within the marketplace. To create a western contemporary dining hall feel, Mexican tiles, wagon-wheel chandeliers and western cowboy icons appear throughout the space, etched in glass and cut out of metal to define the space and separate the various seating areas of the food court. Custom copper light sconces are inset with milk-glass panels to add warm light to the space.

Design: TLHorton Design Inc., Dallas — Tony L. Horton, president; Wayne Keown, project manager West End team: Geena Piwitz Architect/fixturing: TL Horton Design General contractor: B&B Construction, Dallas Furniture: Loewenstein, Pompano Beach, Fla. Flooring/ ceiling/wallcoverings: B&B Construction Laminates: Nevamar, Odenton, Md. Signage/ graphics: TLHorton Design

Photography by Joe Aker, Aker Zvonkovic Photography, Houston

AMC STUDIO 30

HOUSTON

The 110,000-square-foot facility is AMC's first totally themed freestanding theater. The design is based on a studio back lot where guests will feel as though they are on a sound stage. The three theater wings are "sets" themed after movie genres: Cyberspace, Action/Adventure and Animation. The Animation area features "blimp" directional signs in a blue sky with flat clouds, and all architectural features are outlined in black to look like an animation cell. The Action/Adventure area resembles a rain forest with wet leaves, bamboo and rock directional signs. Fiberoptic eyes that change color peer out from behind leaves, and custom-designed carpet represents a river with grass along its banks. Cyberspace features brushed-aluminum walls with a ceiling and floor of the same color. Inside the lobby, black and white clapper directional signs on pulleys show visitors to one of 30 theaters.

Design: Kiku Obata + Company, St. Louis – Kiku Obata, creative director; Kevin Flynn, AIA, architect; Heather Testa, John Scheffel, Gen Obata, Therese Henrekin, Joe Floresca, Liz Sullivan, Lisa Bollmann, Cliff Doucet, Carole Jerome, Alissa Andres and Jonathan Bryant, designers AMC Studio 30 Team: Sam Giordano, vice president of design, development and facilities; Bill Temper, director of architecture; Doug Seibert, director of design and development – south division Credits continued on page. 173.

Photography by Gary Quesada, Clawson, Mich.

WORLD OF DISNEY
LAKE BUENA VISTA, FLA.

With a lakeside location, the new store is nearly as wide as a football field and rises to a 65-foot cupola finished with a Tinkerbell weathervane. Airships at each entrance identify Disney characters in travel around the world, a theme carried throughout the store. Design was inspired by Green & Green architecture, evident in squared light fixtures, Tiffany glass panels above the perimeter fixturing system and a soaring rotunda. Special effects in the great hall include 25-foot-long flying machines and a 45-foot evening-sky ceiling painted with phosphorescent paint and lit with black lights to "shimmer" the stars. Each room is themed for a character or group of characters, including Alice in Wonderland, Snow White, Fairies, Villains and Pleasure Island. Fixtures, in many cases, are Disney-inspired, including a 12-foot-high Mickey silhouette merchandised with purses and accessories, a giant Alice holding plush, a crocodile with shelves and a Pooh tree fixture, among others.

Design: Elkus Manfredi Architects, Boston — David Manfreddi, principal; Walt Disney Imagineering, Burbank, Calif. — John Sircus, vice president and creative director; Burgin Dossett, development manager; Rob Brown, construction manager; Walt Disney Attractions team, Lake Buena Vista, Fla. — Anthony Mancini, director, retail store development, store design and visual merchandising; Johnnie Rush, manager, store planning and design; Kevin Callahan, manager of visual merchandising Architect: Elkus Manfredi Architects Lighting design: Illuminart, Ypsilanti, Mich. General contractor: Hoar Construction, Orlando, Fla. Fixturing: Westco, New York City; Edron, Miami, Fla.; Fetzer, Salt Lake City Furniture: Fetzer, Salt Lake City Ceiling: Marsh Industrial, Birmingham, Ala. Laminates: Avonite, Belen, Minn. Signage/graphics: Bell Industrial, Port Orange, N.J.; Walt Disney Imagineering — John Nelson (murals) Props/decoratives/mannequins/forms: Greneker, Los Angeles; Walt Disney Imagineering (character sculpting)

Photography by Marco Lorenzetti, Chicago

GENE JUAREZ SALON & SPA

TACOMA MALL, TACOMA, WASH.

Architectural forms, bold colors and materials are used to draw mall shoppers into this 8,500-square-foot salon and spa. The two-toned maple floor, laid in broad stripes, creates a wayfinding pattern for direction and orientation. Within the salon, each station resembles a personal vanity with its own mirror and individual wall sconces. Walls are patterned with oversized diamonds and accented with large gold-leaf frames; a fine metal-mesh canopy overhead increases the sense of intimacy.

Design: NBBJ Retail Concepts, Seattle – Donna Davis, principal in charge; Michelle McCormick, project manager; Rysia Suchecka, design principal; Jennifer Mann, designer; George Ostrow, project architect; Leo Raymundo, graphic designer Client team: Michelle Coe, Gene Juarez, Lori Davis, Linda Racknor Architect: NBBJ Retail Concepts, Seattle; Mark Von Walter, Seattle (consulting architect) Visual merchandising consultant: Debbie DeGabrielle, Seattle General contractor: Rafn Construction Co., Seattle Fixturing: Pacific Coast Showcase, Tacoma, Wash. Flooring: Forbo, Hazleton, Pa.; PermaGrain Products, Newtown Square, Pa.; Armstrong, Lancaster, Pa. Ceiling: Armstrong, Lancaster, Pa. Lighting: Lightolier, Fall River, Mass. Laminates: Nevamar, Odenton, Md. Wall coverings: Innovations in Wallcoverings, New York City

Photography by Chris A. Webber, Bothel, Seattle

MASHREQBANK PRIORITY BANKING CENTER

DUBAI, U.A.E.

The objective of this priority banking center is to attract and keep high-net-worth and well-educated individuals as life-long customers by providing highly personalized banking services in a comfortable and sophisticated banking environment. To accommodate the needs of these customers, the center was designed as a place not only to conduct complex banking transactions but also to appeal to non-banking interests. So in addition to private, one-on-one transaction areas, the center was designed with rooms dedicated to fashion (magazines, videos and a private writing desk), sports, business (with multi-media workstation, financial software, magazines and books) and travel, each with its own color scheme. Seminars and lectures on many topics are offered, and valet parking, cappuccino and espresso for all customers.

Design: WalkerGroup/CNI, New York City — Patricia Oris, creative director; Diego Garay, architect; Derick Hudspith, Renata Zednichek, production director Client team: Abdul Aziz, president; Nader Haghighat, executive vice president; Ali Raza, vice president Architect: S.J. Halley Associates, Dubai, U.A.E.

Photography by Faramrz Beheshti, Dubai, U.A.E.

UPS COURIER SERVICES

FIRST CANADIAN PLACE, TORONTO

This new 853-square-foot prototype, intended for worldwide roll-out, needed to create an easily recognizable identity for UPS in the retail market. Graphics readable from a distance were a key factor in communicating the international express mail services that UPS provides. Graphics also encourage self-service, reducing the number of staff required. To eliminate the traditional separation between customer and staff, the circulation plan is open and the sales counter is replaced with a circular work station. Fixtures are modular and interchangeable, for use in a wide variety of floor plans and building types.

Design: Grid/2 Int'l., New York City — Martin Roberts, president; Akka Ma, partner in charge; Christopher Daly, project planner; Betty Chow, Jeffrey Cook, graphic designers; Todd McGregor, Mary Ann Bayton, Ryan Henderson, project team General contractor: Cassidy Construction Ltd., Ottawa, Ont.

Photography by Grid/2 Int'l., New York City

BANCO BANIF

MADRID, SPAIN

This exclusive, private bank has a facade that is opaque during business hours (and transparent at night) to protect the privacy of its high-net-worth customers. Inside, one-on-one consultant offices are designed to project an air of intimacy combined with business, with historical references to personal banking. To lessen distractions, the environment is minimal — full-height paneling, soft lighting, vaulted ceiling and custom furniture — with no art displayed there. Lateral corridors to and from these offices allow customers to exit with minimal contact with other customers. In the waiting area, a green damask sofa offers comfort and adds warmth to the room. A meeting room with a retractable wooden screen allows bankers to hold functions and invite clients to discuss business over a meal.

Design: Retail Planning Associates, Columbus, Ohio — Doug Cheesman, chair; Gerry Postlewaite, account executive; John Cameron, project manager; Edd Johns, retail strategist; Todd Chappell, environmental designer
Banco Banif team: Pedro Alvares Ribiero, Miguel Angel Luna Mansilla; Emilio Anton Architect: Taic Architects, Madrid Furniture: Vitra Espanna, Madrid; B&B Italia, Madrid; Kamen, Madrid Lighting: Erco, Madrid

Photography by RPA, Columbus, Ohio

UMMELINA INTERNATIONAL DAY SPA
SEATTLE

The 5000-square-foot spa is centered around a skylit atrium. The use of wood, glass, stone, concrete, metal, natural fibers and earth-tone colors reflect Ummelina's philosophy of nature combined with the latest spa technologies. Custom fixturing with built-in vitrines, adjustable glass shelving, stained existing concrete and polished terrazzo floors are some of the reclaimed and economic uses of materials. "Petroglyphs" on salvaged teak doors symbolize the nature-inspired environment in each room. "The Desert," a sauna and body treatment area, uses reclaimed cedar timbers, desert sand slate floor and alabaster accent lighting to create a unique dry sauna experience. "The Rainforest" features dark green slate flooring and green accent tiles to represent an abstract forest environment.

Design: GGLO, P.L.L.C., Seattle − William Gaylord, AIA, member-in-charge; Renee Roman, project manager; Julia Brunzell, interior designer Ummelina International Team: Nina Ummel, chief visionary officer Additional Consultants: Mag Secretario, Mag:Design, Seattle; Trina Haines Prawat, Savvy Inc., Seattle; Fixturing: Kinsella Woodworks Co., Seattle Furniture: David Smith & Co., Seattle Flooring: L.M. Schofield, Los Angeles; Dal-Tile, Dallas; Unique Tile, Seattle; American Slate Co., Seattle; Armstrong World Industries, Lancaster, Pa.; Mannington Commercial, Calhoun, Ga.; Karastan/Bigelow, Atlanta Ceiling: Armstrong World Industries, Lancaster, Pa. Lighting: Lightolier, Fall River, Mass.; Basic Source, Rohnert Park, Calif.; Tec Lighting, Chicago Laminates: Pionite Decorative Laminates, Auburn, Maine Wall coverings: Unique Tile (U.S. Ceramic), Seattle; Dal-Tile, Dallas; Ann Sacks Tile, Seattle; Seattle Curtain, Seattle; Duluth Timber Company, Seattle Fabrics: Hemp Textiles International, Bellingham, Wash. Signage: Messenger Sign, Seattle; Peter David Glass Design, Seattle Graphics: Ivey Seright, Seattle; Janine Matthews Design, Seattle Props/decoratives: David Smith & Co., Seattle; Waterdance, Seattle

Photography by Eckert & Eckert, Portland, Ore.

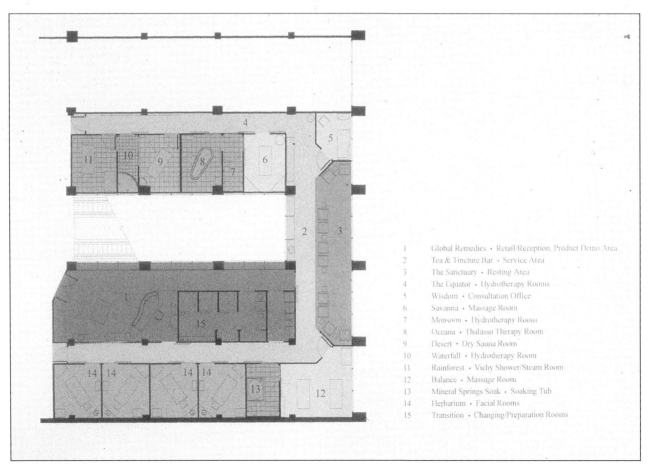

1   Global Remedies • Retail/Reception, Product Demo Area
2   Tea & Tincture Bar • Service Area
3   The Sanctuary • Resting Area
4   The Equator • Hydrotherapy Rooms
5   Wisdom • Consultation Office
6   Savanna • Massage Room
7   Monsoon • Hydrotherapy Room
8   Oceana • Thalasso Therapy Room
9   Desert • Dry Sauna Room
10   Waterfall • Hydrotherapy Room
11   Rainforest • Vichy Shower/Steam Room
12   Balance • Massage Room
13   Mineral Springs Soak • Soaking Tub
14   Herbarium • Facial Rooms
15   Transition • Changing/Preparation Rooms

DICK'S CLOTHING AND SPORTING GOODS

NOTTINGHAM SQUARE, WHITEMARSH, MD.

A value-oriented mass-merchandise sporting goods retailer, Dick's creates visual impact through use of sports-authentic materials and creation of various athletic environments. The golf pro-shop near the cashwrap area, for example, features traditional colors, simulated cherry wood, chandeliers and wall sconces, as well as inexpensive materials that create a wood paneling motif. Other areas include athletic shoes, camping equipment and a hunting and fishing lodge of logs and rough-sawn lumber. Video monitors, 40 of them, are intended to motivate athletes in each respective sport department. Special features include a running track, scaled-down basketball court and Sports Illustrated's first licensed apparel shop.

Design: Horst Design Group, Inc., New York City – Douglas B. Horst, principal-in-charge; Fidel Miro, planning and design director; Cynthia Davidson, colors and materials; Pat Rock, job captain; Merri Reilly, Peter Gerace, production team; Bernhart Rumphorst, lighting design Retailer's team: Ed Stack, president; Bill Colombo, chief operations officer; Gary Solomon, vice president construction; Carol Rueckle, graphic design Architect: Dorsky, Hodgson + Partners, Philadelphia General contractor: Rycon Construction, Pittsburgh Fixturing: Spectrum, Freeport, N.Y.; Northeast United, Vestal, N.Y. Flooring: Ardex, Pittsburgh; Duraflex, Hartford, Conn.; Shaw Commercial, Dalton, Ga. Ceiling: Armstrong, Lancaster, Pa. Lighting: Cooper Lighting, Elk Grove Village, Ill. Laminates: Formica, Cincinnati; Wilsonart, Temple, Texas Signage/mannequins/forms: Spectrum, Freeport, N.Y. (fabrication)

Photography by Gil Amiaga, Southold, N.Y.

JONES NEW YORK COUNTRY OUTLET

WOODBURY COMMON, N.Y.

Created to offer casual and Friday wear to the Jones customer, this outlet store had to maintain the manufacturer's upscale image in an outlet environment. A cherry wood floor and gray walls are embellished with crown moldings and base for a traditional background, while Parson-style tables and leather seating add a contemporary contrast. Residential-style fixturing is made up of prefabricated MDF cabinets with recessed standards in 8- to 10-foot heights and field-applied decorative moldings and drawer inserts.

Design: Visconti Design Associates, Oakland, N.J. – Chris Visconti, owner; Christine Wild, Mike Tully, Anthony Sinochic Retailer's team: Jenifer Mats, director of operations; Howard Buerkle, president; Vincent Micciche, merchandising General contractor: CPM Associates, Brentwood, N.H. Lighting: Lighting Management, New City, N.Y. Stylist: James Andrews, New York City Fixturing: Spectrum, Freeport, N.Y.; CPM Associates (custom fixtures and furniture) Flooring: Buell Harwood Floors, Dallas Mannequins/forms: Spectrum, Freeport, N.Y.

Photography by Frank La Bua, Wyckoff, N.J.

LANDS' END INLET

RICHFIELD, MINN.

The store was designed to be the Lands' End catalog "come to life." At the point of entry, the customer is confronted with an oversized reproduction of two pages from the catalog, and all landscape and lifestyle graphics have been taken from catalog archives. The store offers a residential feel through use of warm tones and a relaxation area where shoppers may sit to peruse the catalog. Standard fixturing was dressed up with wood caps and decorative crown molding. The color palette takes its cue from the land, sea and sky that inspire the merchandise, and the corporate founder's series of quotes, "The Principles of Doing Business," reinforce the link between the store and the catalog.

Design: Retail Planning Associates, Columbus, Ohio – Doug Cheesman, ceo; Peter McIlroy, account executive; Vincent Faiella, project director; Jason Hudson, retail strategist; Mike Torok, environmental designer; Marie Haines, merchandiser/planner; Perry Kotick, lighting designer; Diane Perduk Rambo, color and materials Lands' End Inlet Team: John Mahler, Kris Malmberg, Brad Gillium Flooring: Mannington Commercial, Calhoun, Ga.; Crossville Ceramics, Crossville, Tenn. Laminates: Nevamar International Paper, Odenton, Md.; Wilsonart International, Temple, Texas Special finishes: Tiger Drylac, Reading, Pa. Wall coverings: Pratt & Lambert, Chicago; Innovations in Wallcoverings, New York City; Surface, Beachwood, Ohio; Gilford Wallcoverings, Jeffersonville, Ind. Wall base: Allstate Rubber Corp., Queens, N.Y. Ceiling: Armstrong World Industries, Lancaster, Pa. Furniture: Bernhardt, Lenoir, N.C.; Lowenstein, Pompano Beach, Fla.; Charlotte Company, St. Louis; KI, Green Bay, Wis. Fabric: Brentano, Northbrook, Ill.

Photography by Tom Dubanowich, Columbus, Ohio

RAK'S BUILDING SUPPLY

LOS LUNAS, N.M.

Enlarged from 9,000 square feet to 26,000 square feet, the building supply store now includes a 7,000-square-foot green-house and garden center. Intended to appeal to both the professional trade and do-it-yourself shoppers, Rak's identified paint, hardware and tool lines as growth areas. Red trusses and a perpendicular cornice add dimension to hanging department signs, and the ceiling is painted blue to move eyes down to wall fixtures. To appeal to do-it-yourselfers, graphics are now project- rather than product-oriented.

Design/design and decor fabrication: Programmed Products Corp., Novi, Mich. — Llew M. Reszka, president; John Zafarana, ceo Distribution America team: Jeff Dietrich, interior architect, Richard Tabet, general contractor (Rak's) Architect: Claudio Vigio, Albuquerque, N.M. (exterior) Flooring: Armstrong, Lancaster, Pa. Lighting: Border States Electric, Albuquerque, N.M. Signage: Sunco, Albuquerque, N.M. (exterior signage); Color Arts, Racine, Wis. (window decals) Fixturing: Madix, Terrell, Texas (sales area shelving); Krauter Store Fixtures, Indianapolis (warehouse storage racking); Interlock, Minneapolis (truss system)

Photography by Llew M. Reszka, Novi, Mich.

CHRYSLER GREAT CARS, GREAT TRUCKS

MALL OF AMERICA, BLOOMINGTON, MINN.

The showroom is intended to take the customer on an emotive journey through Chrysler's vision of the future of driving, juxtaposed against the landmarks of the brand's heritage. Vehicles are presented by lifestyle use and brand attributes, and within lifestyle exhibits geared toward their target consumers. Interactive technology abounds in the showroom, including terminals linked to the World Wide Web, a video theater, driving video games and hands-on displays such as the Jeep Wrangler driving simulator. Guests can use the interactive displays to browse Chrysler's full line of products.

Design: Fitch Inc, Worthington, Ohio – Mark Artus, project manager; Christain Davies, Jon Baines and Jacquie Richmond, associate vice presidents; Fred Goode, director; Paul Lycett, Mark Henson, Randy Miller, Steve Smith and Kathleen Goode, senior associates Architect: Gastinger Walker Harden Architects, Kansas City, Mo. Additional Consultants: Ross Roy Communications, Bloomfield Hills, Mich. General Contractor: Nelson Brothers Construction, St.Paul, Minn. Fixturing: Excel Store Fixturing, Toronto Furniture: Vitra, New York City; Knoll, New York City; Wilkhahn, New York City Flooring: Collins & Aikman, Dalton, Ga.; Durkan Carpets, Dalton, Ga.; Permagrain Products, Newton, Pa. Lighting: Time Square, New York City; Lightolier, Fall River, Mass. Fabrics: Spinneybeck Leathers, Amherst, N.Y. Signage: George P. Johnson Company, Detroit Graphics: Aperture, Boston Jeep Simulator: George P. Johnson Company, Detroit AV Technology: Business Television, Detroit Wall coverings: IC/Glidden Paints, Cleveland

Photography by Mark Steele, Fitch Inc., Worthington, Ohio

DESIGN TEX SHOWROOM

NEW YORK CITY

To position the contract textile manufacturer as a design-oriented company, the 2,500-square-foot showroom promotes custom design potentials through providing work space and public access to the computerized loom and CAD studios. Combining a sample library, feature displays, graphic messages, working computerized loom and design studios, the space also houses samples on hooks within easy reach of customers. A grid-frame system allows new graphic panels to be changed easily, and allows fabrics to be featured without sewing.

Design: Lee Stout Inc., New York City — Lee Stout, Cam Lorendo, Leslie Steven, Lynn Campbell Design-Tex team: Tom Hamilton, Susan Lyons, Allan Smith Consultant: Bonnell Design Associates, New York City General contractor: Nucor Construction, New York City Fixturing: Michael Gordon Inc., Paterson, N.J. Furniture: Metro, Burlingame, Calif. Flooring: Interface Flooring, LaGrange, Ga. Lighting: Halo, Elk Grove Village, Ill. Wall coverings/fabrics: Design Tex, New York City Signage: The Sign Co., New York City Props/decoratives: LSI, New York City

Photography by Norman McGrath, New York City

156

HUSH PUPPIES BRAND ROOM

ROCKFORD, MICH.

For Wolverine World Wide's largest and most recognized brand, Fitch developed an 855-square-foot brand room within corporate headquarters. Used for meetings, presentations and tours, this space is designed to create a holistic first impression of the brand for key customers and potential new customers. Wolverine's mission statement is placed prominently on a wall. Natural materials and earthy colors communicate comfort; there is a particular emphasis on lighting to enhance the shoes.

Design: Fitch Inc., Worthington, Ohio – Martin Beck, ceo; J'aime Alexander, project manager; Paul Westrick, retail designer; Alycia Freeman, designer; Maribeth Gatchalian Hush Puppies' team: Jim O'Donovan, executive vice president; Jeff Lewis, director of marketing; Blaine Jungers, president, retail division; Dave Bonney, director, retail division Fixturing: Mock Woodworking, Zanesville, Ohio; Designers Workshop, Columbus, Ohio Flooring: Interface, LaGrange, Ga.; PermaGrain Products, Newtown Square, Pa.

Photography by Mark Steele, Fitch Inc., Worthington, Ohio

THE JOSEPH & FEISS CO. SHOWROOMS

NEW YORK CITY

The 150-year-old Cleveland-based manufacturer wanted to present its new, softer lines to a younger and more affluent audience. Designed to resemble a gracious apartment with sweeping park views, the showroom space presents minimal product displays with the bulk of the line behind doors. Authentic historical details include a fireplace mantle salvaged from a Brooklyn brownstone; an alabaster lighting fixture from the hall of a Manhattan townhouse, Spinneybeck leather furniture, soapstone sconces and a set of eight chandeliers.

Design: Cite Design Corp. — P.J. Casey, president and senior designer; Michael Cooper, creative director; Etienne Locoh-Donou, designer; Anne Marie Brennan, project manager and designer Joseph & Feiss team: Steve Rees, president; Pamela Franklin, office manager; Liz Porter, assistant to president Architect/general contractor: Cite Design Corp. Fixturing: Nationwide Millwork, Bluepoint, N.Y. Furniture: Furniture Consultants, New York City; ICF, New York City Flooring: Desso, Wayne, Pa.; Stone Source, New York City Ceiling: The Cheyenne Co., New York City Lighting: Urban Archaeology, New York City Fabrics: Spinneybeck Leather, Amherst, N.Y. Signage: Green Mountain Graphics, Long Island City, N.Y. Props/decoratives: Cite Home Store, New York City Mannequins/forms: ALU, New York City

Photography by Andrew Garn, New York City

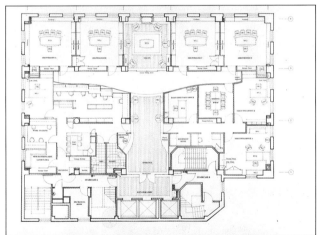

MAX FINKELSTEIN INC. GOODYEAR SHOWROOM
LONG ISLAND CITY, N.Y.

The showroom mirrors the strength, independence and beauty of a sleek automobile. The reception desk is curved and finished in a metal laminate to mirror the shape and treads of a tire and the movement of the road, and the metal cubed ceiling is custom-colored to the Goodyear blue, emulating the freedom of the outdoors. A Goodyear race car is mounted on metal tread plate, creating a decorative and industrial look against the race car to accentuate its vigor and motion. Decorative frames are used around the many existing columns in the building to incorporate them into the industrial design plan.

Design: Milo Kleinberg Design Associates, Inc., New York City — Jeff Kleinberg, Stacey Polavi, Marc Messina Architect: Milo Kleinberg Design Associates, Inc., New York City General Contractor: BFI Fixturing: Rigidized Metals Corp., Buffalo, N.Y., treadplate pattern for display on tire & car Flooring: Graniti Fiandre, Itauca, Ill. Ceiling: Architectural Systems Inc. Lighting: Lightolier, Fall River, Mass. Laminates: Architectural Systems Inc. Props/decoratives: Boston Retail Products (column enclosures), Medford, Mass.

Photography by Peter Mauss, Esto Photographics, Mamaroneck, N.Y.

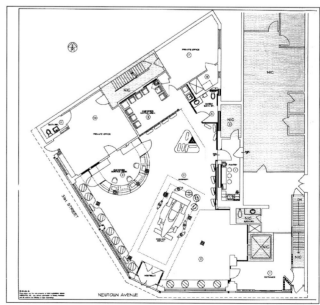

PELLA WINDOWSCAPING CENTER

SCHAUMBERG, ILL.

For this manufacturer of high-end wooden windows, the showroom/retail space needed to inform customers about the quality of Pella's products and provide information and design ideas. Focal points around the space communicate features and services available, as well as interactive technology that allows shoppers to see how windows will look on their own houses. An "inspiration center" offers reference books, project videos and case studies, while an "informational core" provides detail about the anatomy of windows.

Design: Fitch Inc., Worthington, Ohio – Martin Beck, ceo and project manager; Fred Goode, retail designer; Mary Jayne Robey, implementation; Randy Miller, graphics; Kian Kuan, designer Pella team: Sherri Gillette General contractor: Interior Construction Corp., Chicago Fixturing: The Village Woodsmith Inc., Delaware, Ohio Lighting: Lighting Management, New City, N.Y. Graphics: ChromaStudios, Columbus, Ohio

Photography by Mark Steele, Fitch Inc., Worthington, Ohio

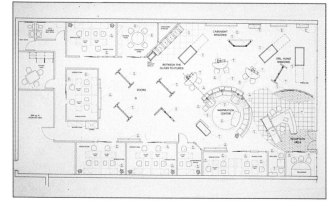

LEADER COMMUNICATIONS
CHICAGO

The 5,000-square-foot showroom is an exhibition and retail center designed to showcase emerging wireless technologies for CellularOne in the Midwest. Retail space is formed by a series of easels with overhead banners that group products, accessories and associated literature. Rolling projection screens open up the central arena space for large-scale events; and manufacturers' exhibits occupy pads below lighting and acoustic clouds hung from the ceiling.

Design: Florian Architects, Chicago Paul Florian, principal, Stephan Wierzbowski, principal; Sergio Guardia, project architect, Lora Delestowski-Wierzbowski, graphic design; Christopher Manfre, architect Client team: Shawn Landgraff, president; Jeff Tottleben, project administrator; Ryan Kutter, project administrator General contractor: ICI Corp., Chicago Laminates: Nevamar, Odenton, Md.; Formica, Cincinnati; Pionite, Auburn, Maine Lighting: Flos, Huntington Station, N.Y.; Lightolier, Fall River, Mass.; Juno, Des Plaines, Ill.; Alkco, Franklin Park, Ill.; Norbert Belfer, Richmond, Ind. Furniture: Vecta, Grand Prairie, Texas (lounge seating); Jacobsen/ICF, New York City Veneers: Marlite, Dover, Ohio

Photography by Barbara Karant, Karant Studios, Chicago

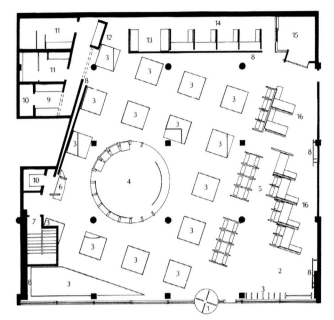

MICROSOFT ENTERTAINMENT STATION

@COMP USA, CONCORDE, CALIF.

This stand-alone fixture is designed to carry a high capacity of merchandise while engaging customers through a monitor that can be seen from a distance. The unit can be connected to a centralized server that can track user activity such as time on and titles chosen; software can be updated, changed or upgraded through this ISDN link.

Design: Retail Planning Associates, Columbus, Ohio — Doug Cheesman, chair; Mike Bills, account executive; Linda Rosine, associate project director; Laura Evans, associate project director; Edd Johns, retail strategist; Conrad Chin, environmental designer; Tim Smith, art director; Diane Rambo, colors and materials; Vince Notaroberto, merchandiser; Perry Kotick, lighting; Adam Limbaugh, visual communication; John Hamlett, Mike Huning, documentation specialists; Dave Linn, implementation specialist Microsoft team: Retail Planning Associates lead by Rebecca Kotch

THE GREAT MALL OF THE GREAT PLAINS
OLATHE, KANSAS

To draw attention and underscore the one-million-square-foot high-quality regional center's value focus, outside entrances feature oversized copyright-free visual images on a metal structure, all of which adhere to stringent visual standards set by the developer, Columbus, Ohio-based Glimcher Realty Trust. In keeping with the conservative feel of the Olathe, Kansas area, the design team decreed that exterior graphics could only be black and white. No taglines are permitted, and the brand name may only take up a small percentage of the entire graphic.

Design: JPRA Architects, Farmington Hills, Mich. – James P. Ryan, president; Rob Stacherski, planner; Eileen Devine, designer; Ron Rae, graphic designer; Dan Sexton, project manager; David Peterhans, design director; Matt Woods, design coordinator Great Mall Team: Glimcher Realty Trust, Columbus, Ohio – Douglas Campbell, vice president and project director; Lawrence Ebel, vice president store planning and design Architect: JPRA Architects, Farmington Hills, Mich. Outside Design Consultants: Ingrid DeOrlow, executive creative director, Ingrid Anderson DeOrlow Ltd, Farmington Hills, Mich.; Charles Senseman, executive creative director, Charles Senseman Company, Detroit General Contractor: Dan Spinosi, Columbus, Ohio Fixturing: M. Lavine Design Workshop, Cold Spring, Minn.; Presentations Plus, Long Lake, Minn.; Universal Display & Design, New York City Furniture: Adele Lewis, Inc., Austerlitz, N.Y.; Blue Moon Gallery, Montgomery, Ohio; Elevations, S. San Francisco, Calif.; M. Lavine Design Workshop, Cold Spring, Minn.; Presentations Plus, Long Lake, Minn. Signage: Air Control Co., Kansas City, Mo. Props/decoratives: Adele Lewis, Inc., Austerlitz, N.Y.; Alvaro Jurado, Detroit; American Balloon Factory Inc., Lee's Summit, Mo.; Blue Moon Gallery, Montgomery, Ohio; Bradbury Barrel, Bridgewater, Maine; Celestial Ironworks, Lawrence, Kansas; Chip Carman, Columbus, Ohio; David Swiatek, Royal Oak, Mich.; Elevations, S. San Francisco, Calif.; FF&E, Richmond, Va.; German Village Antiques, Columbus, Ohio; Greater Images, Kansas City, Mo.; M. Lavine Design Workshop, Cold Spring, Minn.; Mera Vic, Kansas City, Mo.; Niedermaier, Chicago; Universal Display & Design, New York City; Vogue, Whittier, Calif. Mannequins/Forms: Allen Mayer, Ltd., Lake Zurich, Ill.; Elevations, S. San Francisco, Calif.; Vogue, Whittier, Calif. CAD drawings: Caldwell Sarmiento Assoc., Logan, Ohio; Glavan Assoc., Columbus, Ohio Foamboard: Superior Fome Boards Corp., Chicago

Photography by Frank Nash, Detroit

SOURCES

JOSLINS, PARK MEADOWS

Architect: Baxter Hodell Donnelly Preston Inc., Cincinnati Lighting Consultant: Hans Shoop, Myrtle Beach, S.C. General Contractor: Rentenbach Contractors Inc., Knoxville, Tenn. Fixturing: ALU, New York City; R.A.P. Security Inc., Cudahy, Calif.; MET Merchandising, Chicago; Russell William Ltd., Odonton, Md.; Golden Oldies, Flushing, N.Y.; Fall Mountain Furniture, Keene, N.H.; Visual Concepts, Washington, D.C.; YDI, Inc., Chicago; Zero U.S. Corp., Lincoln, R.I.; InterMetro, Wilkes-Barre, Pa.; Niedermaier, Chicago; Europine/Dateline, Bridgeport, N.J.; Vermont Store Fixture Corp., Danby, Vt.; M. Lavine Design Workshop, Inc., Cold Spring, Minn.; Woodworkers of Denver, Denver; Showcase Creations, Graybill, Ind.; Display of Nashville, Nashville, Tenn.; Bruewer Woodwork Mfg., Cincinnati Furniture: Pucci International, New York City; Carol Barnhart, New York City; Niedermaier, Chicago; Ikeru Ltd. Design Workshop, New York City Flooring: Innovative Marble & Tile, Hauppauge, N.Y.; Gabrielli Poured Surfaces, a division of Innovative Marble & Tile, Hauppauge, N.Y.; Tile & Marble Collection, Miami; Mineral Life, Inc., Miami; Milliken, La Grange, Ga.; Shaw, Dalton, Ga., Atlas, Los Angeles; Pucci International, New York City; Bentley Mills, City of Industry, Calif. Ceiling: The Celotex Corp., Tampa Lighting: Osram/Sylvania, Danvers, Mass.; Indy Lighting, Fischers, Ind.; Focal Point, Alsip, Ill.; Voight Lighting Industries, Leonia, N.J.; Ruud Lighting Inc., Racine, Wis.; Mark Lighting Fixtures Co. Inc., Moonachie, N.J.; Halo Lighting Brand Cooper Lighting, Elk Grove Village, Ill.; Pucci International, New York City Laminates: Formica Corporation, Cincinnati; Pionite Decorative Laminates, Auburn, Maine; Nevamar International Paper, Odenton, Md.; Wilsonart International, Temple, Texas Wall Coverings: Design West, Mission Viejo, Calif.; D'Ankha; Gerry Pair; Arton Corp., Atlanta Signage: Adams Sign, Nashville; Allen Signs Graphics, Fine Art and Mirror: Ace Designs Inc., Bristol, Pa.; Rosenbaum Fine Art, Boca Raton, Fla.; Carol Barnhart Inc., New York City; Ikeru Ltd. Design Workshop, New York City Props/Decoratives: Carol Barnhart Inc., New York City; Delectable Display, Carlsbad, Calif.; Patina Arts, City of Industry, Calif.; A&J's Amazin, Napa, Calif.; Greneker, Los Angeles Mannequins/Forms: Bernstein Display, Astoria, N.Y.; Carol Barnhart Inc., New York City; Pucci International, New York City; Goldsmith, Long Island City, N.Y.; Seven Continents, Toronto

REI FLAGSHIP STORE

Lighting Design: Candela, Seattle — Denise Fong, designer General Contractor: GLY Construction, Bellevue, Wash. — Mark Everson, project manager Fixturing: 90 percent of the store fixtures were fabricated by the REI Construction Shop, Renton, Wash., including: 149 gondolas (and 601 units of modular gondola components). Other suppliers included: (merchandising carts, display items) M Lavine Design Workshop Inc., Cold Spring, Minn; (log merchandising supports) That Log Furniture Co., Seattle; (metal components) True Coat Inc., Seattle; (standard apparel floor fixtures) Grand & Benedicts, Portland, Ore.; (custom display fixtures) King Merchandising Concepts Inc., Seattle; and (custom merchandising units) California Decorative Mfg. Inc., Rancho Cucamonga, Calif. Furniture: That Log Furniture Company, Seattle (log benches) Flooring: 5,800 square yards of concrete were poured for the store's main flooring. Other flooring elements included: 6,000 square yards of "Maslon" carpet supplied by Interface Flooring Systems, LaGrange, Ga. 670 square yards of hardwood for specialty departments supplied by Western Hardwoods, Seattle 300 square yards of DLW-Marmorette linoleum for basement-level offices supplied by Dodge-Regupol, Lancaster, Pa. 80 square yards of slate and 80 square yards of tile for restrooms supplied by McKay Granite, Seattle Ceiling: 500,000 board feet of exposed glue-laminate beams supplied by Woodlam Structures, Seattle 10,000 square feet of ceiling tile supplied by Armstrong World Industries, Lancaster, Pa. Lighting: 60-plus fixture types were employed. Suppliers include: (glass refractors, metal-halide lamps) GE Lighting, Cleveland, Ohio; (accent/track lighting, wallwashers) Staff Lighting Corp., Highland, N.Y.; (uplights, floodlights) Kim Lighting, City of Industry, Calif.; (wallwashers) Litecontrol Corp., Hanson, Mass.; (conference and meeting room lighting) Columbia Lighting, Spokane, Wash.; (bollard/lamppost fixtures) Pauluhn, Tearland, Texas Laminates: 55 square yards of countertop laminates supplied by Nevamar, Odenton, Md.; and Wilsonart, Temple, Texas Wallcoverings: 400 square feet of Dodge cork tile, supplied by Dodge-Regupol, Lancaster, Pa. Signage and Graphics Fabrication: 250-plus interior signs including garage signs, departmental identification signs and displays 100 garage structural columns with painted directional and identification signs 60 bicycle wheels for the "gateway" sculpture for the cycling department 11 snowboards, 5 pairs of cross-country skis and 8 pairs of downhill skis for the skiing department gateway Suppliers: (exterior identification signs) National Sign, Seattle; (garage signage, department identification signs, restroom signs, elevator directories) Trade-Marx Sign & Display Corp., Seattle; (exterior banners, bicycle and ski department sculpture "gateways") Koryn Rolstad Studios/Bannerworks Inc., Seattle; (log signs and directories) Doty & Associates, Seattle; (REI Story exhibit) Turner Exhibits, Seattle; (boulders) Marenakos Ornamental Stone, Issaquah, Wash. Props/decoratives: REI Construction Shop, Renton, Wash. Mannequins/forms: REI Construction Shop, Renton, Wash.

AMC STUDIO 30

Architect: Gould Evans Goodman, Kansas City, Mo. Engineers: Engineers Consortium, Leawood, Kansas; Norton + Schmidt Engineers, Kansas City, Mo. General Contractor: MBK Construction, Ltd., Laguna Nigel, Calif. Signage Fabricators: Adcon, Ft. Collins, Colo.; Design Communications, Boston/Orlando; Federal Sign, West Hartford, Conn. Flooring: Bentley Mills, City of Industry, Calif.; Crossville Ceramics, Crossville, Tenn.; Interstyle, Vancouver, Wash.; American Olean Tile Co., Lansdale, Pa.; Innovative Ceramics Inc., Rosewell, Ga.; Florida Tile, Lakeland, Fla.; Graniti Fiandre, Itauca, Ill.; Innovative Marble and Tile, Hauppauge, N.Y.; Forbo Industries Inc, Hazleton, Pa. Wall Coverings: Sherwin Williams, Cleveland Vinyl Base: Armstrong World Industries, Lancaster, Pa.; Allstate Rubber Corp., Queens, N.Y.; Roppe Corporation, Fostoria, Ohio Illustrator for custom wall covering: Bill Mayer, Decatur, Ga. Fabric Wallcovering: DesignTex Inc, New York City Decorative Coatings: Duroplex, Houston; Crafton Plus, Dallas; Ferroxtone, Dallas; Zolatone, N. Billerica, Mass. Wood Veneer: Ventec Veneer Technologies Ltd., Chicago Ceiling Tiles: USG Interiors Inc., Chicago Solid Surface: DuPont Corian, Wilmington, Del.; Gibralter National Corporation, Detroit; Formica Corporation, Cincinnati Plastic Laminates: Formica Corporation, Cincinnati; Nevamar International Paper, Odenton, Md.; Wilsonart International, Temple, Texas; Pionite Decorative Laminates, Auburn, Maine; Abet Laminati, Englewood, N.J.; Arborite, Hazleton, Pa. Lighting: Halo Lighting Brand Cooper Lighting, Elk Grove Village, Ill.; Isolite, San Luis Obispo, Calif.; Sure-Lites Brand Cooper Lighting, Elk Grove Village, Ill.; Infinity Display Inc, Owings Mills, Md.; H.E. Williams Inc., Carthage, Mo.; BEGA/US, Carpinteria, Calif.; Metalux Brand Cooper Lighting, Americus, Ga.; Dayton Showcase Company, Dayton, Ohio; Prescolite Moldcast, San Leandro, Calif.; Visa Lighting Corp., Milwaukee; Lightolier, Fall River, Mass.; Lighting Services Inc., Stony Point, N.Y.; Foscarini, Italy; Lumark Lighting Brand Cooper Lighting, Vicksburg, Miss.; Hydrel, Sylmar, Calif.; McGraw-Edison Brand Cooper Lighting, Vicksburg, Miss.; Sentinel Diversified Industries Inc., E. Farmingdale, N.Y.

INDEX OF DESIGNERS